THE ELEMENTS OF JAZZ

THE ELEMENTS OF JAZZ

BY TOM WETMORE

OVERTURE PRESS
NEW YORK

"Be hungry for the music."
Harold Mabern

Contents

THE SKILLS CHECKLIST

FOR PIANISTS

ON LISTENING

ADVANCED MATERIAL AND CONCEPTS

APPENDICES

IDEAS TO ADD

Introduction

The "Elements of Jazz"

The title of this book is derived from the celebrated "little book" by William Strunk Jr. and E. B. White, *The Elements of Style*. If you don't know it, pick up a copy; any time spent on it will be time well spent. Ostensibly, *The Elements of Style* is a rule book for writers—11 rules of usage, 11 principles of composition, a "few matters of form," and 21 "reminders." The rules are simple and declarative, and despite the directness of the book's presentation, and the extreme brand of concision employed throughout, the book is simply fun to read. These are the fundamental elements, and they're presented with elegance and style. Both a reference and a piece of art in itself, the little book seems to be almost as important to the art of writing as pencil and paper.

One of the things I really dig about the book is how "standard" it has become. I'm fascinated by standards; and I'm especially fascinated by standards that "give you the goods" and give them to you straight. The rules, simply written, easy to understand and apply, and sufficiently definitive to give the practitioner the security of an un-shakable foundation from which he or she can confidently explore new and exciting territory of creation, both well-informed and rigorous.

The book is also short, and I like that. I've had my share of instructional books in my day. Learning from a book has always felt a little off to me—somewhat unsatis-fying and less than genuine. It's definitely not necessary. That has been proven hundreds of times in the history of music, especially jazz, with its amazing aural tradition.

Jazz is hard

Before the rules, there are some basic conceptual points I'd like to discuss. First, mastering jazz will require the absorption and mastery of considerable information. When I was young, just starting to dip my feet into im-provisation, I spent a lot of time trying to improvise on my own, sitting at the piano by myself. I got some results, but with little guidance and little experience my improvi-sations were never particularly pleasant to listen to. Then someone showed me—or I discovered it on my own, I don't recall which—the concept of pentatonic scales. All of a sudden, I couldn't play a wrong note; all of them sounded just right.

I'd listen to Miles Davis's Kind of Blue record and wail on D minor and Eb minor pentatonics and ask myself, "What's so hard about this whole improvisation thing?" Before that, I'd read and heard all those stories of jazzmen of yore poring over record players to diligently transcribe gems, some of them even transcribing bits and pieces of solos from the radio, without even the tiny benefit of lis-tening twice—and all that stuff just sounded like so much work. But now, armed with my five transcendental notes,

I felt like I had found the golden ticket; I could bypass all that stuff and just master my fingers and those five notes. After that, all I had to do was wait for the phone to ring and the gigs to flow my way. For all my ears could tell, the only difference between Cannonball and me was that he could play pentatonics faster. This isn't to say I didn't take practicing seriously at that time. Nothing could be further from the truth. I was enthralled by jazz and couldn't get enough; and my fingers were constantly on the piano.

Then my ears developed. I realized, man, that there really was a huge difference between Cannonball and me. All those notes that sounded like pentatonics were so much more. And even the ones that were simple pentatonics had so much more meaning and creativity in them because of all the work he put into it. About how much he knew and had mastery of what he was doing.

The moral of the story is you just can't take the simple route to playing good jazz. It may feel like it sometimes, and that feeling can actually have benefits—confidence is important—but it is important to keep in mind the simple reality that there's nothing easy about playing jazz; it will take a long time to get attain even a marginal level of mastery.

But I want to emphasize that I'm not saying that it should be hard. I'm certainly not saying it should be painful. Those are the last things it should be. Every time you sit down to connect with your instrument, whether in a practice session, at a jam session or at a live gig, you want to be enjoying it; you want to be embracing it and relishing every opportunity you can reconnect with our instrument and reconnect with the music.

There will be times when this is simply impossible. Don't feel bad if you don't want to practice. Diligence is difficult to maintain. Music is a craft and craft requires work. But be careful never to get in such a rut that practicing becomes a chore, something you want to avoid. If you feel yourself getting to that point, drop the pressure on yourself and step back. When you sit down the next time—whenever that may be—you will have a renewed vigor. And I have little doubt that the time spent practicing when you're really into it and passionate about it is ten times more productive and meaningful than the time spent practicing out of simple obligation.

Again, the moral of the story is that you have to master lots of information to play effectively. This is quite a problem with jazz. A problem and a blessing. The complexity of the requisite language makes for an exceedingly difficult process to become an adequate performer (and a correspondingly difficult process to become an adequate listener), but it allows for heavier, deeper music, music with more angles and more intricacies—music that rewards the listener even after hundreds of repeated listenings.

There was a time jazz was much closer to popular music. That was before jazz musicians started to more or less perform for other musicians; when dancing left the picture; when it became self-conscious. I won't get into the debate on whether this been a bane or a boon, but it's the way it is. Jazz has become art music, almost exclusively.

Who This Book is For

This book is not a beginner's manual or "learn jazz quick" type tome. It is meant for the serious student of jazz who wants to get beyond the basics and delve into the nitty gritty of serious artistry. I use both words "student" and "seriously" very loosely. Though I feel this little book could (and probably should) be read by younger students (college and earlier), it is meant to be on the level of those already possessing a certain level of training who could benefit from some kind of organizational framework to "put the pieces together." And by seriously, I simply mean those people that take the music as an important part of their life and raise it above the level of "playing around" to the level of creating "art." Now, those are very difficult to define terms (especially art), and I am in no way qualified to provide a definition, but suffice it to say if you take your career in music and are in it for the sake of creating something truly creative, this book is for you.

I myself have had difficulty putting everything together. There are just so many varied skills necessary to playing this music adequately that it's almost impossible to keep solid balance. For instance, I would find myself trying to master odd-meters, focusing so much on playing in 7 and 9 and 11 and the like and not play a blues for months at a time. Then I'd get called for a gig and feel uncomfortable playing what other people wanted to play.

This book is most applicable to those focusing on so-called "traditional jazz," which I simply mean the strain of jazz directly descendant of blues, bop, post-bop and related styles. Further, it is most direct toward the standard jazz repertoire—but I hope the guidelines provided here are far more universal. Personally, I have found myself wandering increasingly far from this style of improvised music, focusing more and more on original compositions and other forms of performance that stray from the type of forms used in traditional jazz (chord changes, blues, song forms, etc.). There are many extraordinary musicians that most classify under the "jazz" umbrella that focus entirely on such more modern styles. Some of these completely eschew the notion that learning jazz standards or bebop vocabulary is required or even beneficial to a musician's development. This is an entirely legitimate viewpoint, and one I subscribe to in many respects. But for the purposes of this book, the ideal reader is one who wants to advance in some type of progression from this traditional.

I don't want to give the impression that I'm talking about "old" music when I mean the kind that stems from traditional jazz. That's not what I mean at all. I personally don't believe that jazz should be considered "museum" music, as it has started to evolve into—a trend I loathe. But there are a wide variety of truly cutting edge musicians that are the end products of the evolution of what I am now calling "traditional" jazz. Modern musicians like Brad Mehldau, Chris Potter, Kurt Rosenwinkel—all true innovators in a modern style—are the offshoots of this tradition, and this method. All these men, and many others like them, got to where they were because they diligently mastered the concepts I present in these pages.

This book is also aimed at those looking for a particular kind of elegance and style in their playing. I am not espousing that particular style of musical creations, but for the purposes of this book, maintaining a certain amount of controlled creativity, the kind that results from extensive "honing" of the music—which should be considered a true craft to be worked on extensively. This is most certainly not the only way to think about music and the development of personal style. The last thing I want to do is to make rules, as if they're infallible.

On Rules

These aren't rules, and I am ashamed of myself for calling them such in this book. But despite my shame, I still know that, though they don't really exist, that having some rules will be helpful for adding some type of structure to one's development as a musician. As soon as a rule is written down (after being thought about in some kind of contemplative way) it becomes a standard against which one can compare his or her actions. And even before the rules are applied to actual playing (I'm talking about while this book is read or directly after, when the student is pondering what pieces of advice to take to heart and which ones to dismiss entirely—not to mention the ones that elicit a response of disgust or hatred) they can form something of a framework to your development. Just remember I put down some rules. I wish I didn't have to—I myself realize how silly it seems for an improviser to make a list of rules (especially a list as in depth and specific as this one), but I'm glad I did it, if for nothing else than the fact that it adds some structure.

Jazz, in some ways, is much easier than other forms of improvised music to teach. There is a fairly well defined vocabulary and theoretical framework. And there have even been quite a few common "themes" that have developed in recent decades that have, to some extent, "standardized" jazz education. This is quite good in some ways, because it has made the core of jazz (the blues-derived stuff that swings) much easier to teach—and this has helped the raw number of practitioners of jazz increase. On the other hand, with codification and standardization one often ends up with something of a watered down product.

I am no jazz purist. I grew up in Newburyport, Massachusetts, and when I was a kid I was more interested in listening to predominantly white rock bands than classic jazz records. There's nothing particularly positive or negative about these facts, but what's important is that I recognize that my background is simply different than someone like Mulgrew Miller, for instance, who grew up much earlier and in a much different social and even geographical situation, in Memphis Tennessee in in the 1950s and 60s. Influenced mostly by classic jazz musicians like Oscar Peterson, it is much more understandable that Miller would be drawn to and excel in the bluesier, more swinging aesthetic than someone like me.

This book is about getting the best results while still maintaining the joy of jazz.

Fundamental Principles

1. Listen.

Listen to music. Listen to live performances. Listen to recordings. Listen to ten albums in a day. Listen to one tune for a week. Listen to one chorus of your favorite solo for an hour a day. Listen to your most hated chorus for two hours a day. Three hours a day. Listen to the sound of your voice. Listen to others. Listen to speech. Listen to babies. Listen to birds. Listen to footsteps. Listen to traffic.

The point is, listen to everything, not just music. This should go without saying, but I mention it here because its importance cannot be overstated. Too often the primary weapon in a musician's arsenal is the brain. This probably shouldn't be particularly surprising, since such a large amount of a great deal of the "material" or "techniques" acquired or developed in the course of jazz education or training are derived from "thinking" about music, or being "taught" a concept from a teacher, then learning (with our brains) to "apply" it to our instrument.

2. Keep music a positive experience, and contribute positively.

Never lose the joy that brought you to jazz in the first place. With all the daily work involved in learning jazz—the grind of practice, the never-ending droves of vocabulary and repertoire—it's easy to lose track of the more spiritual dimensions of the music. Jazz is difficult, and mastering it takes incredible persistence and consistency. But it is important to always maintain a strictly positive, even ecstatic, relationship with the music. Spending time with your instrument should be a healing, cathartic experience. Even as you maintain a rigorous routine and comprehensive overall strategy for improving, never lose touch with the pleasure of playing jazz.

The pursuit of jazz is a serious undertaking, one that requires real, consistent work. I present a bevy of rules in this book to give some structure to the undertaking, because it is so easy to get overwhelmed with the mass of things that are necessary for becoming a competent jazz musician. I strongly believe these rules will help you get where you want to go faster. But, still, I encourage you ignore any rule that takes away from the joy of playing music.

3. Set goals and make concrete plans for attaining them.

Make sure you know want to go, because nearly impossible to get anywhere without knowing it. Write down your goals—as specifically as you can manage. Don't skimp on this rule. Studies have shown that those people who go through the very simple act of writing down their goals have a astonishingly higher chance of achieving those goals.

Especially in a field such as jazz, in which individuality and freedom are cherished, the issues of discipline and focus are paramount. Setting clear and attainable goals will allow for a systematic approach to reaching them. There is only a finite amount of time that can be spent with your instrument, or listening to music, or doing any of the other things important for developing as a musician. As a result,

Your goals should be both long term and intermediate term. Know where you want to be by the end of the day, the week, the month, the year, etc. Not only will this force you to take stock of your position on a regular basis—allowing you to assess how the actions you are currently taking are helping or hurting your chances of attaining your goals—but you will also be able to maintain a framework allowing you to feel the satisfaction of the many intermediate landmarks along your progression.

The degree to which you write out your goals, and the amount of time you dedicate to such an enterprise, is entirely up to you. You probably don't want to spend a half an hour a day writing and re-writing endless lists of goals, but it is probably worth the effort to keep a few pages in your notebook dedicated at all times to a dynamic list of goals on various timescales.

Imagine what you'd like to be like as a musician in one year. List out the aspects of your playing you'd like to see improved, and in which ways. This can be a liberating experience, and it can provide invaluable structure to your daily practice. Too often we find ourselves buried within our daily routines. We head to the practice room for days on end, getting obsessive about very specific things. We may spend four hours a day going down lists of tunes, playing them, improvising on them… really digging into them. We may become so involved in such a project that it's almost all we do for weeks and weeks.

Then, after some time has passed, we may be put in an uncomfortable situation. Maybe a situation where we have to do something like sight-reading, which really requires a regular commitment of practice time in order to stay on the top of one's game. Or we may be asked to play in a style we haven't touched in months—but a style we have wanted to improve on.

This kind of imbalance happens in the life of a musician all the time. We get too caught up in the short term goals that we simply have our mind at a certain time, losing track of the big picture—and we can easily forget all about certain aspects of our playing (and life) that are also very important. Keeping a list of goals, both long term and short term, assures that we are on track, and if we stray too far from our mission, at least we will be reminded of it on a fairly regular basis.

4.   *Compete only with yourself.*

If you're harboring secret aspirations to be better than all the other jazz musicians out there, it's probably best to change your outlook. As you spend more time in the jazz community—and I mean the real world of jazz, not conservatory and college music programs—you will realize that such notions as "better" and "best" are counterproductive in almost all cases. Jazz is such a personal undertaking, and there are so many ways to approach it, that comparisons between musicians make little sense. One pianist may be able to play faster while the other may play with more harmonic intricacy. Even if every measurable aspect of a certain musician's playing is off the charts, it means little if their playing lacks heart, or soul, or some kind of creative spark. The point is that you just can't quantify creativity, so comparisons and competition should be avoided.

Now, there are some isolated circumstances in which amiable competition can be useful. In jam sessions comprised of similarly minded and similarly skilled players, good-natured contests can spark new ideas and propel your playing into territory you might not otherwise probe in the more serene, solitary sphere of the practice room. But on a large scale, competition is almost always damaging.

In educational settings in particular, competition can be intense and extensive, leading to a musical culture that is counterproductive to creativity. On a typical night, students surreptitiously peer into others' practice rooms, desperately fearful of hearing anything too advanced. This fear of inferiority often leads to feelings of inadequacy, which make becoming an artist much more difficult. At the same time, when mistakes are heard emanating from their peers' practice rooms, students breathe a sigh of relief, having been granted temporary relief from their fear of falling behind.

The repercussions from such attitudes can be pervasive. Students and other young jazz musicians often fear being heard, and they fear performing in front of others. They're not entirely comfortable in their practice rooms, and as a result they make deleterious alterations in their practice routines. Instead of focusing on weaknesses, or playing repetitively and slowly to attain accuracy and technical facility, most students in such circumstances spend most of their practice time trying to play fast and sound impressive—hampering their progress considerably. Learn to avoid such neuroses and you will open up a more effective, and more pleasurable, path to effective music making.

5. *Find influences everywhere.*

Some jazz musicians don't stray too far from the traditional jazz idiom in their listening, but you'll do yourself a disservice if you confine yourself to a strictly jazz-only musical diet. The jazz tradition, despite its relatively short period of existence, has an unbelievable mount of great music, and you could easily spend a lifetime studying recordings and scores in the accepted canon. And you would have barely scratched the surface. But such listening and study could also badly suffocate you, cutting you off from ideas and inspirations that would otherwise enrich your musical vision.

Jazz provides an ideal introduction to the world of improvised music. The tradition is there. The infrastructure is there. The educational resources are there. And the music has an ability to really inspire younger people to think independently and come up with their own ideas of where they want to go musically. But the music scene has become too diverse and interesting for it to be acceptable to shut your ears to the musical developments that have occurred and are occurring outside of the jazz world.

The best jazz musicians—including the ones the get the most paid work opportunities—are the ones that can easily adapt to many different situations—R&B, Soul, Rock, Indie, etc. Explorations into other genres and styles can provide added perspective to your jazz playing, and they can also provide access to expanded worlds of musicians with whom you can collaborate and learn from. And with the relative shrinking of the jazz industry, it is an unfortunate fact of life that one must expand beyond the strictly jazz world if one wishes to make a living.

6. *Master awareness and control. Then just play.*

Though complete awareness and control can be deleterious to spontaneous creativity, you must first master them before throwing them away. Many of the greatest jazz musicians cite a blissful state of unawareness as the highest ideal in the course of improvisation, and such a state can indeed result in inspired improvisations. But it's important not to confuse this species of sublime detachment, which requires years of diligent training and practice, from the detachment born of inattentiveness or lack of rigor.

We all go on autopilot from time to time. We lose focus or our mind drifts away, and we let our body—or, more specifically, our fingers—do the work on their own, with little input from our brains. Our fingers have no problem doing the work on their own. Autopilot is the enemy of good musicianship. If you don't have awareness of what you're doing, you aren't going to be able to effectively improve your playing.

In jazz it is all too easy to fall into the trap of feeling accomplished and inspired in our playing without working through that essential stage of solidifying all the fundamentals. Because nothing really sounds bad when we stay within a few basic frameworks of harmony or rhythm, many jazz musicians fall into the habit of letting their fingers fly around the instrument with little discipline. Most of the time, this yields reasonably good sounding results. Thus, we fool ourselves into believing we have control and we think we're being artistic, while in reality we are reinforcing bad habits and widening a disconnect between our true creative selves and the actual music we create.

Thus, we must spend a certain amount of practice time making sure that we are aware—rigidly aware—of what we are doing. Sing along with yourself. Focus intently on hearing absolutely everything comes out of your instrument, careful to detect when something comes out you didn't specifically intend to come out. If you catch yourself getting carried away with flashy runs—your fingers taking over—slow down or stop or stop immediately. Bad habits are hard to break, so this won't be easy, but your work will pay significant dividends.

You should also strive for awareness of your place within a group or performance situation. Hear and feel what you are doing yourself, but take special care to discern your place within the overall group sound. It isn't necessary to hear everything; it's impossible to keep track of every instrument in a group at the same time. But it is important to develop a deeper awareness of the collective intricacies and nuances of a group performance. Keep in mind that an end goal is to know what you are doing and know how it fits in with what others are playing. And when that awareness is strong, you can make the last step of good music, which is making sure your contribution is positive.

7. Get started.

You can't practice unless you start practicing. The best plan in the world, the most insightfully concocted and lucidly formulated, is useless until you sit down and execute it. Every musician is regularly faced—probably more often than we would be comfortable admitting, even to ourselves—with difficulties in getting down to business and starting our daily routines.

Even after going through great lengths to carve out the time to practice from our otherwise busy lives, we still habitually find reasons to avoid starting. Maybe we just don't feel like it, or perhaps whatever else we're doing at the moment just feels little easier or a little more interesting at the time. These and a number of other factors make the initial step to start practicing all the more difficult.

So the single most important goal is to sit down, get in the practice room, and get down to business. After you start playing, everything changes; it won't seem like a chore anymore. In his book, *Effortless Mastery*, Kenny Warner proposes a useful method he calls the "five minute method." "Just tell yourself you are only going to practice for five minutes," Kenny says. "Every time you begin, be sure to stop after five minutes, regardless of what's been accomplished." By telling yourself you'll only be working for five minutes, you make it easier to sit down and get moving. But you will find, in almost all cases, that "five minutes come ten, ten becomes twenty, and so on."[1]

If you just sit down and start working, the desire will come. You'll want to keep at it. So do whatever you have to do and just get yourself in the room with your instrument with the absolute minimum of delay.

8. Put in the time.

The time you spend with your instrument is not a vacation, and it is not playtime. It shouldn't be time to fool

---

[1] Kenny Werner, *Effortless Mastery*, (New Albany, IN: Aebersold, 1996), p. 177.

around. To make real advances, it is necessary to be organized, detailed, and goal-oriented. Despite all this, however, the most important thing in advancing as a musician is to put in the time, no matter how it is spent.

I advocate maintaining a written out daily regimen to your practicing, but if you haven't written one don't let that stop you from practicing. Sticking to the plan will often feel distasteful or boring. You just might not feel like doing what you probably "should" be doing. In the long term, the real problem to be addressed in learning jazz is to put in the time.

It is essential to avoid any negative feelings associated with playing music. Music must always remain a positive experience for you, so if you don't want to follow the regimen, or if you don't even have a regimen, don't let that stop you. Every rule in this book must be unceremoniously discarded if it holds you back in any way from spending time with your instrument.

We all have spent a great deal of time hesitating before starting a practice session because we are nagged by subconscious (and often conscious) fear that we just don't know what we're going to do when we sit down with our instruments. There are just so many things that need to be covered to become an adequate jazz musician that keeping your head around what the thing you should be working on now is an overwhelming question.

The amount of time I've spent thinking about what I should be practicing would probably be staggering if it were at all possible to calculate it. The same goes with the amount of time I've spent feeling bad about practicing the

There are literally millions of things a jazz musician must master. This amount of material requires incredible amounts of work, even if practice sessions are organized and focused. But it's important to remember that learning to play jazz is a marathon, not a sprint. As much as we want to think to ourselves that practicing 8-10 hours a day will have us playing with Herbie at Carnegie Hall in a couple years, it just doesn't work that way. But if you practice as consistently as you can for as long as you can, you maintain your passion, you develop over a long period of time, and slowly but surely you become the player you'd always dreamt of being.

Practicing incredible hours each day can still be your goal, even if it doesn't send you to Carnegie Hall immediately. But what must be avoided at all cost is the kind of practice that makes you feel bad—or gets you into a rut in which you avoid the instrument. That's the real killer. When you spend weeks or months, or even years, away from the instrument because of some kind of "falling out" you had with the music, that's the truly bad stuff. But you can play most days—even if you're often unfocused or undisciplined—then you will turn into an excellent player in the long run.

As the years go by, it becomes harder and harder to find the time, and the inspiration to get going has a tendency to become more difficult to muster. The last thing we need when our inspiration is low is an added sense of guilt for not working on the "right" stuff, or apprehension over not knowing where to start. So if you're putting in the time, you're on your way.

9. *Don't make music the only thing in your life.*

Jazz is a serious art form. It is a craft requiring seriousness of purpose, love, and consistent dedication and work. But jazz shouldn't be the only thing in your life.

We have been presented with a romanticized image of the great musicians as existential warriors fighting a romantic war in the name of artistic achievement. In this fairy tale, the great masters lived and breathed nothing but art. Surely they didn't get bogged down by such petty distractions as relaxing, watching television, sleeping late, or any of the other litany of things that make us feel so guilty about avoiding our instruments.

The truth is that the great jazz musicians of the past were in almost every case just as lazy as any of the rest of us. Maybe they felt like they should be practicing more than they did—plagued by the same nagging sense of guilt that affects us—or maybe they didn't even care. But let's just clear our minds right now of the idea that Charlie Parker' put in eight hours every day of life, or four hours, or even one hour. He didn't. How about Miles Davis? I don't think so.

Despite what you may have been told, or what you may have imagined, learning jazz is not about superhuman feats of technique or all-consuming practicing marathons. We don't have to play catch up with the greats; we just have to keep our goals straight, our plans straight, and consistently get to work, practice session after practice session, gig after gig, until we find our true voice and an ability to competently express it. But to attain such goals requires balance, in both music and your life overall.

What we don't need is the hysterical, competition-based culture I've seen in many places in jazz education. I've been particularly saddened by the John Coltrane paradigm, which holds up Trane's legendary practice habits as the ideal to be striven for—the standard against which all other practice habits are to be compared—setting up young musicians to either burn out trying to duplicate them or feel depressed for failing to muster the energy to try.

I would never say anything bad about Coltrane. He's one of history's best, a true genius, and there are endless reasons to look up to him. But the idea that we must duplicate the things he did, the way he did them, in order to reach the highest levels of artistry has developed into one of the most damaging fallacies in jazz.

Droves of young jazz musicians go to bed dreaming about what it would be like to Coltrane. The momentousness of his accomplishments and the passion with which he strove to attain them can be a steady source of inspiration. But let's not forget about the profoundly negative consequences of Trane's life choices.

On a human level, when we put aside the tremendous artistic output he left us with, the man was a mess. He had difficulty relating to others personally or functioning effectively in the practical matters of his life. For most of his life, he found solace in dangerous and addictive drugs. And he died young. He wasn't a balanced individual, and this imbalance in his life likely led to his early departure.

Coltrane is an ideal example of someone who made music his entire life, and the extreme nature of his devotion led him to live an extreme and unhealthy life. If deep down in your heart you feel that you'd rather have utter imbalance in your life in exchange for musical greatness, perhaps the Coltrane model is right for you. But do not make such a life decision without understanding the consequences. And know that life like Trane's is not a requirement to attain musical greatness; it is far more often a detriment.

A better lesson to be learned from Coltrane's life may have been the manner in which he structured his career in the long term. A meticulous student, Coltrane set goals and made plans for attaining them. He mastered bebop language so he could expand into his "sheets of sounds" period. He explored every technical and musical aspect of his instrument so that he could have to facility to expand into the area of free jazz in a way that was informed and artistic. This diligence and focus on the long term, as seen through the overall arc of his career, should be the lesson taken from Coltrane, not the fanatical nature of his work ethic.

Virtually all the true legends that have made a lasting impact on the world of jazz today are exceedingly decent and balanced individuals. They have time for their friends and time for their family, and with few exceptions they are gracious and excited to help younger musicians find their path and develop into mature artists.

Your primary long term goals should be to get better, maintain your artistry, and to stick with it. If you obsess too much on short term goals, you will burn out. Maintain a balanced and healthy life, and your heart as well as your soul will thank you.

10. Don't quit.

If you want to become an excellent or even a great musician, it's not about how much talent you have. It's not about getting started when you're young or having the right teacher or going to music school. It's not even about being a practice room rat, spending every waking hour shedding (though it helps). It's about sticking with it over the long haul. It's about to taking jazz seriously as an art and understanding that it takes real work and dedication to create real music that's worth listening to by other people. The only thing left is for you to keep at it.

You don't necessarily have to practice four or six or eight hours a day. You'd be surprised how many great musicians practice less than that. Remember, if you don't practice for a week, and for one week you practice four hours, after that two week span, your really only practicing two hours a day. Likewise, if you practice two hours a day and take a week off, that's only one hour a day. The point is that you'd be surprised how much the time adds up when you are consistent, even if you do less work every day. And trust me, the best professionals go days, weeks, and months without practicing.

But there is one thing no great musician (or great anything) has ever done before attaining greatness: quit. If you are sick of practicing, stop practicing. If you are sick of listening to jazz, stop listening to jazz. But don't despair. And don't think that just because you take a break that you've fallen off a train that you can't get back on. Every great musician has gone through extended periods away from the music, and I'd wager nearly all of them came back better because of it.

Not to sound depressing, but every year you don't quit should be cause for celebration, because it isn't easy to do. I know how hard it can be to stick with it. Especially in times of economic trouble, there are countless forces working against the arts. Not just financial, but societal as well. A life in the arts requires extensive time away from the traditional workplace, and those outside of the arts world, despite their best intensions, almost always have a difficult time understanding the value of our work.

Because so much of the process takes place alone, in a practice room or in one's home, often with no outward indications of accomplishment, it can often be a battle to justify the time spent doing something that most people feel has little practical impact on the world. But despite the largely marginalized status jazz and other art forms have been reduced to,

Also, don't feel that if you take on another career, even a full time one, that you have necessarily given up on being a jazz artist. It's certainly more difficult to attain your goals without considerable time to devote to it, but it can still be done as long as you stick with it for the long run. And remember that it is never too late. The incredible power of consistency and determination will make every difference in the world, and as long as you don't quit, you will make it.

Principles of Practice

1. Keep a schedule.

It is important to maintain a targeted approach to practicing, and to maintain such an approach requires organization, discipline, and consistency. The best way I've found to keep such organization is to write out a specific daily regimen or routine—essentially a list of things I'm going to work on and the amount of time I'm going to work on them. This regimen can, and should, be reassessed and modified regularly, based on your changing short-term and long-term goals, but it should always remain a centerpiece of your daily practice.

I recommend preparing a few different routines, each for a specific situation as dictated by the circumstances of the practice session—most importantly, my level of enthusiasm for practicing and the amount of time available for practice. Personally, I like to keep a four-hour regimen—the specific breakdown of which varies regularly—as my ideal minimum. If I can go down the list and check off each point, I feel great about my day. And if I still have plenty of stamina after that, any additional work is a bonus.

But keeping up such a regimen can be challenging, especially when motivation or time runs low. If you can physically bring yourself to the instrument, it can be surprisingly easy to complete such a routine, because the pure joy of playing almost always subsumes any feelings of laziness you may feel before getting down to business. But in some situations, such as a particularly busy day, when the demands of life have already sapped your vitality, an intimidating checklist scare you off from sitting down to practice at all. Such fears can easily lead to feelings of frustration or even depression, both of which make it even more difficult to sit down and play.

What I like to do now is keep various "backup" lists, for the times when for whatever reason I can't complete my ideal routine. I have a certain regimen for when I only have two hours, or one, or even 20 minutes. The simple fact that I planned ahead and put effort into actively thinking about the best way to use my time in these situations gives me satisfaction that when I have to use those lists, that I have made meaningful progress toward attaining my long term goals.

The more specific you can make your schedule the better. Going through four points for 20 minutes each can give you much more momentum and enjoyment, for instance, than 1 point for an hour. Such detail can also allow you to more rigorously plan for addressing the many specific aspects of your playing you may wish to improve. However, if being so meticulous stresses you out, forget it and just make a more general routine (one hour technique, one hour repertoire, etc.). For more specific information on how to compose your own practice routine, see the appendices and the companion website.

2. *Keep yourself honest.*

Without honest evaluation, progress is essentially impossible. Do yourself a favor and make self-evaluation a central part of your life, not just in music but all aspects of life. You can easily be deceived into thinking you worked more than you really did, which can easily lead to an impaired ability to make progress. It's not as glamorous as sitting down and just playing, but honest self-reflection can be the key ingredient to meaningful progress in your music.

While you're at it, don't pay attention to how much other people work—or say they work. There's no way to quantify how much work you're doing without using a timer and keeping some kind of journal or log. Most people don't. They may say they practice four hours a day when they really spend four hours at the music building or in a practice room, far from all of it spent actually playing their instrument. Or it could simply mean they spent four hours not doing something else, when in fact much of that time could have been truly spent eating, walking around, talking, staring at the piano keyboard, talking on the phone, checking email—any number of things.

This happens at music schools all the time. Students linger in hallways of music buildings chatting when they would be better served cocooned in an actual practice room. Hanging out is far too large a part of the music school culture, and it stands in the way of getting good work done. You shouldn't entirely cut out the social aspects of music making, but you should certainly make sure to avoid any illusions about how much work you're actually doing. From this perspective, keeping a log of how much work you actually do can be an eye-opening experience.

Keep a notebook.

Practicing jazz is a mostly solitary process, and since there so little structure surrounding the pursuit of music, it's important to add that structure yourself. Keeping a journal of what you accomplish each day will add an invaluable framework to your musical process. There's no reason to have false illusions about how much work you really do. It hurts our ability to accurately assess or strengths and weakness, thus hampering our ability to take appropriate action to address them.

A journal should include more than a record of what you have done. I spend very little time recording what I actually did. Rather, I use the journal as a play to compile all of my goals and specific routines I have developed to structure my practice sessions and overall goals. I have lists of tunes that I know, and lists of those I don't. I have musical scribblings of various pieces of vocabulary I want to work into my playing. It has it all.

The central goal is to streamline everything you do, making the path of most productivity the same as the path of least resistance. In short, you want to make it easy to do the right thing. I don't want to do a bunch of writing in the middle of making music. That's a disturbance, and it's tedious. So anything I can do to make it quick and easy to make journal entries makes the whole process better.

Perhaps the greatest advantage to keeping a journal is to simply keep track of your progress, and to know how much you really worked. Combined with a timer, you can

If your daily practice routine includes, for instance, 20 minutes of technical exercise and 20 minutes of practicing repertoire, you can easily put these items on a list and simply check off item as you complete them. If you spend extra time on a particular item, you can easily jot it down.

You might say that the journal is unnecessary—that you know can just remember in your mind all the things you need to do, but give it a try. A notebook is better.

Use a timer.

Regular use of a timer will add a much-needed level objectivity to your practice sessions. Honesty is necessary to get better—especially in assessing how much work we are really doing. A timer will fill our need to rise about our own perceptions about the work we are doing and the time we are wasting, because these perceptions are often deeply flawed.

A timer can also help you a good perspective about how you are balancing the material you're working on. We don't want to be unnecessarily obsessive about perfect balance in our practicing—freedom is a big part of jazz, and we don't want to lose track of it—but honesty is essential, and if we want to advance meaningfully we need to be honest. The good news is that when you are completely honest with yourself, and only "count" the actual minutes spend doing real, quantifiable work, your daily "requirement" of time can be greatly reduced. By this I mean that your 2 hours will be equal to what many would call 4 hours.

So if the idea of stopping to timer every time you get up to get a glass of water, or even get up in the room to stretch your back, because amount of time you can tell yourself (and others) that you practice will be greatly reduced, don't worry about it. Yes, the hours will go down, but that's OK. You will have the confidence that the time you're counting is real, and the work you're doing is rigorous, and that you're doing the best thing you can to make tangible advances.

Record.

Technology is too good and affordable not to be recording yourself on a regular basis. Not once or twice a year, or even once a month. You should be recording yourself constantly. Performances, jam sessions, and especially practice sessions. Every day would be great, but every week would be good. As much as you think you know how you sound, you'll never know until you hear a recording of yourself. Not only should you record, you should record often.

By listening back to a recording you can really evaluate yourself in ways you never would without a recording. Recording can be especially useful in giving you a picture of what your rhythm sounds like to others. Everyone thinks his or her rhythm and feel are strong. When the groove starts to get strained or awkward or out of sync, the natural inclination is to think it's the other guy's fault. Even if you're the one that's rushing, it feels to you like the others are dragging behinds. It's entirely natural because of the nature of rhythm feel entirely like where you feel the pulse to be is where it truly is in reality. Anything different than the pulse you perceive yourself seems entirely wrong due to the very nature of our perceptions. There's nothing quite like listening to a recording to get a sense how much your perceptions can be different than the truth.

In addition to keeping you honest, and revealing another perspective of the perception of your playing, recording can also add a level of focus to moments of your practice sessions that can be invaluable. How many times have you played a gig and when it comes to your time to solo you manage to come up with something you'd never thought of in a practice session. For me, this type of epiphany usually leads me to play far simpler, and with far fewer notes, in a live performance than what I normally do in practice sessions. When you know you only have a few minutes to craft a solo, to build a story, your attention and creativity is focused much more on each measure and each chorus, and this focus on real artistry an really bring together so much of what you're capable of doing. In practice, we're so locked in very specific, small picture goals that we don't spend as much time truly creating the kind of truly artistic playing "worthy" of a live performance or recording.

When a recording device is rolling, however, an extra edge is added, whether in a performance for an audience, a private rehearsal with a group, or a solitary practice session.. Just knowing that the sounds coming from the instrument are being committed to recording, and knowing that it will be heard, even if it's only by yourself, there is an extra something that inches your playing closer to the realm of "performance" rather than just practice.

Another benefit to recording your playing is the ability to go back and "fetch" a particular moment—a spontaneous piece of melodic or rhythmic vocabulary, for instance—which can easily be broken down and worked into your practice going forward. Such a concept can also be expanded to composition. It's amazing how much great material comes out of us when we just sit down and start playing our instruments. Many times, our spontaneous improvisations are more lively, interesting, and beautiful than the stuff we labor over through painstaking revisions before committing to paper. But too often we aren't ready with a pencil and paper to record our brilliant ideas as they come. And if we do have a paper, we're often too lazy or involved in the actual playing to take the time and effort to write it down. Recording your composing sessions, or just having a portable recording device (most modern smartphones will just work fine in a pinch)

When you're truly relaxed, and truly in the zone on a particular song, eventually you will find new areas of music that you wouldn't have found otherwise. This is important and true. But if that's all you do, there's a disconnect, and something will be missing in your playing. You can get into the habit of not worrying about what a solo really is. You're not going to be able to play like that in a performance situation.

A potential downfall of such an approach is an excess of recorded material, which could become impractical to review. Recordings are useless unless someone listens to them. Sometimes it takes three hours to review a one-hour recording, if you're paying good attention to it. And when it takes that long, it's just too easy to say, "Screw it, it's not worth it." I wouldn't argue too much with you if you wanted to say that. So, somehow you have to balance the ideas of recording too much and recording too little.

You have to come up with your own system of recording. It's to your advantage to start getting over the technical hindrances to the recording situation. None of your ideas are lost.

See the appendices or the companion website for specific information about various portable recorders appropriate for this purpose.

3. *Attack weaknesses.*

You're only as good as your worst note. A concert is only as good as the worst tune, or the worst chorus, or the worst measure. As an artist, you should strive for proficiency and confidence in all the situations you'll be asked to be a part of. This means that you have to be ready for the stuff you fear the most. The tough chords, the tough tempos (fast and slow), the tough tunes, the tough styles—the tough everything.

Most of the time, we simply fake our way through the tough stuff. This is in many ways an essential part of being a professional. We will never know ever single tune, and we will never be masters of every style or tempo, so a certain ability to just "get through" the more difficult moments is an integral part of the job. When a tough chord comes around, artfully placed silence almost always sounds good. When you're not sure about the chord changes, generalizing the form can work wonders. There are a whole slew of tactics that can be employed if necessary.

But as an artist, do you really want to dread every time that tough chord roles around? Do you want to be on the bandstand and live in fear that the bandleader will call a tune at a tempo, or in a style, that makes you uncomfortable? No, that's not satisfying, and it's not conducive to artistry. You want to have such questions eliminated from your mind and have no worries. That way, the only thing that matters is the actual creative spark of performance. And that is where real musical beauty comes from.

It is often difficult to convince jazz musicians to weight their practice time toward weaknesses. After all, most of us were originally attracted to jazz because it allowed and encouraged us to do what we wanted to, as opposed to what the notes on classical sheet music told us to do. Rarely does a person particularly desire to do what is difficult, because it is less pleasurable.

By focusing the majority of your practicing on weakness you open yourself up to the swiftest and most satisfying rewards. Such efforts are best executed within a highly organized framework. Make the identification and evaluation of weaknesses a central part of your regular self-assessment. Include lists of weaknesses in your practice journal and make a habit of checking in on them to check on your progress.

As always, playing music must stay a positive and fulfilling experience at times, so doing unpleasant things should be avoided. But if you could inspire a real passion for improvement, the pursuit of betterment of weakness can become profoundly pleasurable. Try to develop an attitude a proactive, aggressive attitude toward weaknesses. It should give you pleasure and personal satisfaction to attack them.

Of course, we can't work on weaknesses only. If everyone did that, no one would attain true greatness in their areas of passion because they'd be spending all their time on things they don't do too well. So a good amount of your practice time should also be spent on the relatively strong aspects of your playing that you'd like to improve. But when you are working on strengths, it is best to find some aspects those that are weaknesses.

If you're great at playing modal tunes—say, playing a never-ending D minor chord for hundreds of bars—you might want to focus more on playing material with more dynamic harmonic structures. If you want to be known for incredible chops or expressive ability on modal tunes, look for a weakness in your modal playing that you can work on. If you just turn on the metronome and say, "I'm going to play D Dorian for 15 minutes before I stop," then you'll most likely just practice the same ingrained patterns and pet licks your fingers have already committed somewhat to muscle memory. If your playing improves using this method, it won't be very much. It is much better spending your time working things you don't' already have mastered.

It feels good to play things you play well, but to make real progress it is more important to spend time focusing on the weaknesses in your playing. An artist needs the encouragement and satisfaction of hearing something that genuinely sounds good coming out of their instrument, rather than tediously laboring through exercises and the like, that are likely not very pleasing on the ear.

4. Separate practice and performance.

Practice should be your time for making honest assessments of your abilities, making plans to address your weaknesses, and taking focused actions to improve the specific areas of your playing that need work. Gigs and jam sessions, on the other hand, should your main venues for putting everything together—where you can forget about all the self-assessment and specific tactics and just play. Though a certain amount of overlap between the two is inevitable, you must recognize that practice and performance are different things.

For some jazz musicians, practicing consists of little more than playing through tunes, beginning to end, perhaps accompanied by a play along recording, with little thought put into specific goals or focused strategies. It's easy to slip into his kind of practicing because it feels good, and it's satisfying when what you're practicing actually sounds good immediately, as playing through tunes often does. Exercise or drills—especially when you're focusing on weaknesses—are much less satisfying from this perspective.

On one hand it is important in practice to imitate real performance situations, to prepare yourself for the big show. Without such work, it would be difficult to prepare yourself for the real moment of performance when an audience is present. But keep in mind that there are many things you can't do if all you do in practice sessions is play as if you are performing for an audience. You can't pay nearly as much attention to the smaller details—the specific vocabulary, the targeted weakness that you can attack during a practice session.

The real key is to make sure you are aware of when you are practicing and when you are performing. You can perform by yourself in the practice room. This means playing music as if it is a self-contained piece of art meant to be appreciated as such, even if only you or your recording device are the audience there to appreciate it. This can be profoundly fulfilling, and it can be useful both practically and spiritually.

Jam sessions, whether at a club or in a university music building, are essential for gaining real-world training and experience in the skills necessary to be a professional jazz musician. They also keep you connected to an integral part of the jazz tradition. But make sure that you still have the time to do real, serious practicing as well. Jam sessions and gigs are your chance to forget all the things you've worked on in the practice room and just play. In certain situations they are also the place for experimentation, or acquiring new perspectives that you can later take into the practice room to develop new ideas and skills. But without serious and solitary time in reflection and focused work, jam sessions and gigs are not enough.

Work to gain an awareness of when you're practicing, when you're performing, and when you're just fooling around. All are parts of the life of a jazz musician, but maintaining awareness of how much and how effectively you do each one will help you in the long run to meaningfully develop as a musician.

5. *Always be ready to play.*

If you get a call for a gig, be ready to take it and feel good about it. If someone tells you about a great jam session, be ready to go to it and feel good about it. If someone simply asks you to "play something" for them, or with them, be ready play and feel good about it.

Above all else, your primary goal is to have the ability play music creatively and artistically in performance situations. But keep in mind that this isn't just a long-term goal. The process has no end: there will never be a day when you can sit back and say you're done, that you've attained your goal. So while you should maintain a long-term perspective of where you are and where you're going, remember that you should be ready to perform at all times.

One way to make yourself ready is to know what tunes you'll play in various situations. I can't tell you how many times I've been in jam sessions in which someone asks the " so what do you want to play" question, after which we all just look stand there and look at each other with a blank stare. It's not because we don't know any tunes; we know plenty. It's because it's so easy to forget which tunes we know. So be ready, without hesitation, to call the tunes you're most ready to play.

Make a list, and separate it into categories. If someone wants a blues, be ready with your favorite. If it's time for an up-tempo tune, be prepared with one you're comfortable with. Go right down all the common categories of tunes, tempos, and styles, and be ready with what you would like to play in a performance situation. Aim for tunes that are well known but aren't overplayed. Everyone knows "Autumn Leaves," for instance, but not everyone is always excited to play it. It doesn't have to be a long list, just be prepared for the most likely situations that you will be presented with. And don't forget about solo playing. You're a musician, so you don't want to be dependent on being in a group to be able to express yourself.

You also need to practice the act of "turning on" your performance mode. Allot a certain amount of practice time to imitating performance conditions, and do everything you can to do it accurately. Don't play a solo longer than you would in a real performance, and don't let yourself get carried away with practicing patterns or other vocabulary. Give your performances some kind of beginning, middle, and end. Recording yourself can go a long way in keeping you focused, and it can give to feeling of having an audience.

Ask yourself regularly if you're ready to perform in front of an audience. If you're working on a particular aspect of your playing, don't move on from it until you have the ability to do it in an actual performance. As a jazz musician, being ready for anything should be something you feel in your bones. Cultivate this attitude, and while you're doing so, remember that there is never a need to feel ashamed of your playing. Eliminate any fear of being exposed for your inadequacies. Learning jazz is a long process, and you will likely never feel like you have become an entirely complete musician. Like every other jazz musician, you will always have weaknesses, so work to be ready to perform at all times despite them.

6. Avoid crutches.

Musical crutches help us to "stand up" in situations when we normally wouldn't be able to. When we have weaknesses in one area, relative to another, they help us from completely falling down. And they also limit us from attaining real progress in the long run. We become dependent on them, and whenever we are dependent on anything it restricts our ability to become strong and capable artists.

We want to avoid crutches, because crutches hold us back. Though they make us feel like we can stand up and move, without them we can't, and the listener can tell, even if we can't. Especially early on in our development, the thrill of sounding good, or at least sounding better than we did before

7. Respect muscle memory, and beware of "finger playing."

I think every jazz musician at one point or another—pianists especially—have experienced this problem. Even if unaware, this occurs for everyone. It's boring to slow down. It's boring to restrict yourself to playing the notes you know, the ones you have mastered, the ones you've played enough so that you have full control over them. And to some extent, it's all out wrong to restrict yourself is such away. After all, if you only play notes you've played before, you'll never play new notes! And if there's one thing that's essential to the process of playing music it's that you must constantly move forward.

But, problems really start to arise when you let your fingers do too much of the playing for you. Your fingers have a mind of their own, and if you let them get out of control they'll be moving much more than your mind, or ears, can process. And more importantly, they'll be moving beyond your whole soul's capacity to be involved. They'll leave even the create part of you behind and there will be less connection between the music coming out of the instrument and the creative force within you. In other words, the music won't really be coming from you in the deepest sense; it will be light and less meaningful.

Surprisingly few musicians are aware of the power of muscle memory. Muscle memory—at least in the simplistic for I use, applied specifically to piano playing—is the body's ability to remember a repetitive action and be able to repeat it without

8.   *Know what you're going to practice next.*

Ernest Hemingway once explained his method of avoiding writer's block in an interview with The Paris Review: "Always stop while you are going good and don't think about it or worry about it until you start to write the next day. That way your subconscious will work on it all the time. But if you think about it consciously or worry about it you will kill it and your brain will be tired before you start."

I think Hemingway's method can be easily adapted for use by jazz musicians. Do your best to end your practice sessions on a high note, when you are feeling good about your playing and excited about what you're going to next. And try not to stop unless you know specifically what you're going to work on when you sit down for your next practice session.

This will be much easier if you keep written down schedule or regimen. In such a case you will always know what you'll do first when sit down, because it will be the first time on your list. But in case you can't or haven't established such a habit, take a lesson from Hemingway and stop in the middle of the last thing you're working on. Then the next day, you can simply pick up where you left off.

9.   *Know what you're going to listen to next.*

Just like practicing, it is important to know precisely what you're going to listen to the next time you get down to it. This is probably much easier for some than others. For me, finding something I truly want to listen to can be fairly difficult. I listen so much, and have listened to so much, that the decision of what to listen to can be dizzying.

Sometimes I look at what I've been listening to recently and I'm just not excited to turn it on. I look at what at my collection for what I "should" be listening to, for learning purposes, and I don't find anything that excites me. Like most people, I can only focus for a certain amount of time before my mind moves on to something else. So if I can't find something to listen to that will move me, I sometimes move on to do something else.

Keep in your notebook a list of recordings you want to focus on. Always have enough recordings, and enough "fresh" ones, to ensure you'll never be stumped when you're the time comes for serious listening. Update the list regularly, keeping you in line with your long term goals and ensuring your listening doesn't become stale.

10. Compose, compose regularly, and compose quickly.

There are those in jazz history who have made extraordinary names for themselves almost exclusively through their interpretations of the standard jazz repertoire. But these musicians come from a different era, and it doesn't make much sense to compare yourself to them. You simply must compose to be a serious jazz artist.

There is are hordes of traditional jazz players capable of attacking the standard jazz repertory with vigor, skill, and breathtaking facility. Some of these musicians have solid careers, but only the most exceptional can make a career playing nothing but jazz standards. Unless your approach to interpretation is so profoundly radical that it will significantly alter the way people look at jazz, there are little practical or even musical prospects for a jazz musician who doesn't compose original tunes. Professionally, original compositions allow you to distinguish yourself from the pack faceless masses and carve out an audience that is responds to your individual creative voice.

Even more important are the litany of creative benefits to regular composing—not least of which is the ability to use your compositions as a forum to develop your ideas. Things are just a little more permanent when they're written down. No matter how much confidence you have for your own ability to remember what you played, your memory pales in comparison to a pencil and paper. Composing on a regular basis allows you to record your ideas regularly, committing them to a particular form, and giving them a level of permanence that allows them to be manipulated and abstracted.

On composing fast

You don't always have to write fast, but you certainly shouldn't make a habit of writing slowly. The most significant biggest impediment to composing is the inertia. We often feel that composing should be a slow and meticulous process. After all, it seems as if one of the central distinctions between composition and improvisation is the very fact that composition is slow and improvisation is fast. As a result, we often fall into the trap of making a point of slowing down when we compose, making sure that whatever we commit to paper is "better" or "more refined" than the music that flows out of ourselves easily and naturally. But the second guessing and over-revision resulting from this approach stands firmly in your way to getting your music down on the page. The skills are inside of you—let them out.

The best way to break free of this thinking is to compose quickly, using specific goals. Give yourself an hour to write a composition, for example. Don't worry about how good or bad it is. This can the biggest hindrance to getting ideas down on the page. Keep in mind two things: 1) you can always make changes later and 2) your ideas are almost always better as they come out naturally, without excessive tweaking.

You will also be more productive this way. Almost all of us have at least once in our lives observed that we get exponentially more productivity out of ourselves when faced with a deadline. Try to remember back to when you were assigned essays in school. When given two weeks to do an assignment, we almost always leave it to the end, just as we would if we had been given only one week from the beginning. Sometimes the last hour or so before the big deadlines sees more productivity than the all other time since the assignment combined. For this and other reasons I strongly support the idea of setting deadlines for your compositions, and making them tight.

On composing regularly

If you compose every day, your subconscious will become accustomed to it. Remember that the mind's subconscious performs far more work than the conscious part. It does work you aren't aware of, and if you get in the consistent habit and routines, the unconscious will attack problems when you're away from the instrument and present solutions when you return.

Make your best effort not to skip days in your writing routine. Just like there are exponential gains to sticking to consistency (even if you only work for five minutes at a time), there are significant drop-offs to falling out of the habit. I'm don't advocate limiting your composing to just five minutes a day, but if even that were your routine, and you were able to firmly entrenched yourself in the rhythm of brisk composition for that time, in just a few months you would likely have composed a prolific amount of material. And maintaining the daily routine will the process easier, smoother, and more satisfying.

11. Add positively to the music.

Take a step back once in a while and take an objective look at your playing, asking yourself whether what you're doing is really adding positively to the music. The question isn't whether you sound good—whether your voicings are pretty, or your rhythm is hip, or your solos are burning—but whether you're making the music better. Focus less on what kind of technical feats you can accomplish and redirect that energy toward the simple goal of contributing to overall artistry of the performance. This is where true artistry and meaningful music begins.

You don't have to drill this idea—it's easy enough to grasp the first time—but you should not lose sight of it. A central goal of my method is to develop your habits, so that you never have to worry about rules. So try to take this one to heart.

12. Play for real.

Don't fool around with music. When you sit down to play, do it for real. If you spend part of your practice time mindlessly noodling around the instrument, it will become all the easier to slip into such a trance in performance time. This doesn't mean that you can't sit down and play without a specific plan or goal. Sitting down without a plan can be a good way to connect with the instrument on a spiritual or instinctual level, leaving the intellectual mind behind and focusing on something closer to pure creation.

But when you do this, make sure you're not doing it out of laziness or to kill time until you have a better idea. Commit yourself to the music you're playing. Close your eyes if it helps. Even the notes you're not sure about, the one's you don't want to control, the ones that are meant to surprise you when they come out, should be considered sacred.

Principles of Style

1. Understand phrasing.

A musical phrase is like a sentence in English. If constructed well, a good phrase is long enough to clearly express your point without the clutter of wasted words. Aim at constructing phrases that say what you want to say with out saying much. And, like with written sentences, use punctuation to give your sentences definitive endings. Be aware of the listener, and try to understand that they can't comprehend too much at one time. Even avid jazz fans need breaks in the content to let them gather their thoughts and fully absorb what you're throwing at them. Endless phrases with no breaks or pauses are the mark of an inexperienced improviser, and even the most casual listener can tell.

Be aware, as well, of how you group your sentences into a larger structure. Sentences can be grouped into paragraphs, just like musical phrases can be grouped in more developed statements. A chorus of blues is a common unit of structure, a particular 8 bars in a 32 bar form, like rhythm changes. Imagining opening a book, or even a magazine article, and being greeted with page after page text with neither a period nor a paragraph break. This is how the listener feels when a jazz musician charges headfirst into an entire solo without any pauses, or any breaths, barreling through chorus after chorus without leaving anything tangible for the listener to grasp onto.

Some believe it's not the musician's responsibility to make things easy for the listener. Even if you believe this, the ability to craft uncluttered, intelligible musical can do nothing but advance your playing overall. It makes you more focused and aware of your own ideas, and it provides you with essential skills with which to craft more thoughtful and creative art.

And if you can master the ability to construct clear phrases and situate them within a logical musical structure, you will also be in a far better position to explore more unconventional and unrestricted methods of creativity. Once you've strengthened your phrasing, you will be in a better, more informed position to throw it away.

Look to your favorite recordings for the ultimate resource for learning phrasing. There are infinite subtleties to this art, making phrasing a difficult thing to teach, and to learn. But a solid foundation in listening to quality recordings will get you on your way.

2. Pay special attention to phrase endings.

Phrase endings stick out in the mind of the listener more than anything else in the course of a solo. An inspired improvisation can easily be spoiled by a clumsy, vague ending. Conversely, an uninspired, nebulous phrase—even one plagued with obvious blunders—can be elegantly salvaged with a confident, forceful ending.

Nobody plays clear, meaningful musical phrases all the time. We wouldn't be pushing ourselves enough beyond what is comfortable if we played everything perfectly the first time— and our art would suffer because of it. So we must do our best to walk the line between what is comfortable and what is bold. As a result, there will be times when our playing gets lost in a cloud, our ideas are unclear, or our attempts at creativity simply fall flat. In these cases, the ability to wrap up our ideas with confidence can go a long way toward maintaining our composure and creativity.

Actively work to build up your vocabulary of phrase endings. Specifically compile them, write them down, and practice them. Repeat them on their own and practice them in the context of actual tunes. It may seem like cheating, but it's no different than learning standard greetings or farewells. It's just another part of learning to speak the language of improvised music.

3. *Aim for melodies that sing.*

A good test of a good melody is if it can be sung as a melody. It's certainly not a requirement, but it's good to keep it in mind once in a while. Melodies with a singing, lyrical quality connect with listeners in a way that more angular, ornate melodies do not. Most jazz instruments, especially in the hands of a capable improviser with even modest technical ability, can do things far beyond the reach of the human voice. They can play with speed and precision, and they can make singularly angular intervallic leaps.

It's important to find a balance between these two kinds of melodies—which I will loosely refer to as "lyrical" and "instrumental." They are both important. A saxophonist should play the instrument in a manner that takes advantage of its unique attributes, like its ability to make wide intervallic leaps on a dime. Likewise, a like a pianist should take advantage the instrument's many unique attributes, like its ability to play multiple notes simultaneously, or to play with incredible speed and precision. Just make sure you don't get too carried away with what you're body is doing with the instrument, and be sure to check in with the vocal, singable nature of your improvisations on a regular basis.

4. It's better to play less than more.

The tendency for many musicians, especially less experienced ones, is to play too many notes. Fight against this inclination. With the pressure of spontaneous creation with little or no safety net, not to mention the natural inclination to want to impress the audience and fellow musicians, it is only natural to play a lot of notes, and to play them fast. But more often than not, flurries of notes are overwhelming and confused. We get carried away in the moment and play more notes than we can adequately control or even comprehend. If there are so many notes that we can't discern a clear line or phrase, it is probably not as artistic as it could be. A good rule of thumb is this: if you can sing it, you're not playing too much.

5. It's better to end phrases too early than too late.

Your main goal is to connect with listeners. To do this you must craft statements that are meaningful and can be effectively communicated to the listener in a comprehensible way. It's not necessary for everything you play to be easily heard or understood, but be careful not to craft phrases so long that they become cluttered or confused. When in doubt, err on the side of concision.

6. *It's better anticipate chords than play to them late.*

Unless you really know what you're doing, try not arrive at a particular harmonic change late. In other words, if you're playing a ii-V-I progression, don't make it a habit of letting the ii chord hang over the barline into second measure. Playing chord changes late can convey a sense of hesitation or lack of control, and in the hands of a less experienced musician it can add muddiness and confusion to a performance. Some of the best players do this, but until you have a better grasp on what you're doing, opt for anticipation rather than playing late.

When comping, one of the best ways to add forward rhythmic thrust is to anticipate a chord change. The best illustration of this occurs in "Red Garland style" comping, which usually consists of playing chords on the upbeats (the "ands") of beats 2 and 4. In this case, whenever the upbeat of beat for comes around, is it proper to anticipate the chord that is written for the *next* measure. These anticipated chords boost the feeling of moving forward in the music and give it an authentic sense of swing.

7. *Be aware of the rhythm you're playing.*

Fully absorb the feeling of melodic lines in all the reasonable rhythmic subdivisions. Fully assimilate the sound and feeling of playing quarter note lines, quarter note triplet lines, sixteenth note lines, and so on—and do it for all tempos. There's no room for wishy-washy rhythm in good jazz. Play each applicable subdivision repeatedly, with the metronome. Make sure that you can attain the right feel—that you can make the rhythms dance with the beat, and make them swing. Be especially careful when you get to the faster subdivisions.

A common approach to building excitement in a solo is to start out playing only a few, sparsely distributed notes, leaving ample space for the music to breath. Then, as the solo builds, the quantity and speed of notes gradually increase until they're flying from your fingers as fast as you can get them out. Passion and emotion runs high, and the lines get faster and faster. Excitement builds, listeners sit up in their chairs to take notice, and some pretty inspired music can take place. As musicians, we often dream of these moments, and when we attend live performances, these moments make us say to ourselves, "Wow, I wish I could do that."

But if you're not too careful, frantic moments like these will often lead you lose track of the rhythmic value of the notes. Especially for shorter lines—a few measures length, for instance we often simply play as fast as we can, leaving traditional subdivision behind. The notes aren't triplets, or sixteenth notes—they're simply a bunch of fast notes that fill up a few measures. Everybody does this from time to time, and it can be effective in the right situation. But if we push too far, and we lose the basic sense of the rhythm of the notes, we can easily get lost within the measures, and lost within the framework of the overall tune.

After you've truly mastered the traditional subdivisions—including the very fast ones—you will be far better equipped for the freer rhythmic explorations. Staying disciplined in your training in typical rhythmic subdivisions will give you a strong foundation that you can easily fall back on in the course of performance. If we don't have a completely ingrained feel of all the "safe" rhythmic subdivision, it will be far more difficult to situate ourselves if we venture outside of such subdivisions.

Leaving traditional rhythmic subdivisions behind in order explore rhythmic material with little relevance to the basic meter of the tune is common to the very best jazz musicians, but is to be approached with caution by the developing musician. Many of the best musicians play considerable notes, for considerable amounts of time, that don't conform to any typical, rigid category of notated rhythmic values. They're not eighth notes, nor sixteenths, nor any other rhythmic value you'll find in a standard music theory textbook.

Just look at a published Keith Jarrett transcription. You might see 11 notes in the space of one half notes in one measure, then 17 notes in the space of one quarter note in the next. Keith isn't doing math; he is letting his creativity run free without conscious restriction from the actual meter of the tune. The results can be transcendent. But such explorations are not for the beginner; they can indeed be counterproductive to learning to play good jazz.

You need a very firm foundation in the basic meter of the tune, as well as all the traditional subdivisions, before you can take such rhythmic voyages. You must truly feel what 4/4 feels like—or whatever meter you're playing in—and you must feel, without thinking about it, what four measures feels like, or what eight measures feels like, and so on. Your basic sense of rhythm must be so solid that you can detach your mind from the tune's basic pulse, while somehow maintaining that pulse without thinking about it, playing it, or hearing it. Only then will it be feasible to liberate yourself from the pulse and still be able to find your way back.

If we don't have that fundamental pulse deeply ingrained, when we stray away from the steady tick of the basic rhythm, we might get too enamored or attached to the new rhythm we are superimposing on top of it. And when that happens, and the venture outside of the basic pulse comes to an end, if our fundamental feel is not perfect we will come back and not know where we are.

For the developing musician, the biggest trap we want to avoid is not knowing when we are truly straying away from the beat, throwing out notes in passion, with little more than faith that we will come back from the flight on the right beat, and when we are playing fast in a controlled way. As with most things in jazz, this problem requires extensive practice and repetitions to develop. The goal is to think about these things and be aware of them in practice so that we can forget about them in performance.

8. Develop a sense of rhythmic form.

A tune can be separated into various subdivisions in its basic rhythmic form. A 12-bar blues for instance, can be separated into three four-bar divisions. A 32-bar form can be similarly divided. Even a one-chord vamp, when performed with a group, is almost always naturally divided into various rhythmic groupings. The drummer will basically outline four-bar or eight-bar cycles, for instance.

As a jazz musician, you must develop a feel for such rhythmic forms as second nature. They must be automatic, so that your brain can be better spent on other aspects of creativity. Having a true feel for these underlying macro rhythms will free you to go on much more interesting explorations and still be able to return to the basic cycles that are allowing the band to stay together.

You don't want to be counting in the middle of a performance. The more complex the music gets, especially as you being to play with more advanced musicians, the more difficult it will become to keep track of the form. It becomes harder to count each measure because of the increasing levels of rhythmic, harmonic, and melodic abstraction that the various members of the band apply to the performance. You may not be able to fall back on harmonic cues because other members of the band may not be playing the harmony—or they may be abstracting it so much you can't hear it. There may be so many polyrhythms flying around that you simply can't count each measure. And if there are no melodic cues to help you situation yourself, you will likely have little else to fall back on but your instinctual feel for rhythmic form.

To develop this, take special care to pay attention to the great bands you listen to on recordings, noting what kind of signals you hear from the band that they may be using to subtly communicate with each other.

9. *Recognize contrasts, and be ready to exploit them.*

Loosely, what I'm talking about are opposites: loud vs. soft, complex vs. simple, long vs. short—the list is endless. I'm not trying to be trite, but I think it is worth extra meditation. You need to be aware of the extremes so you don't get too caught up in meandering around in the middle. Even in the course of performing one tune, or one solo, you can embrace extremes and embrace contrasts. After all, contrasts are dynamic, and they are interesting, pushing the music forward and giving it a feeling of motion and worth.

Look for all the different contrasts that are littered through performances and recordings: long vs. short, straightforward vs. abstract, modern vs. traditional, loud vs. quiet, fast vs. slow, high versus low (register), dense orchestration vs. sparse orchestrations, staying close to the chords vs. expanding out from the chords—the list is never-ending. Being aware of such things, and actively searching for techniques to take advantage of them, will better allow you to infuse your music with variety and surprise.

10. Breathe.

Be careful not to throw out too many notes, or too many extended melodic lines, without taking a breath (literally or figuratively). Audiences are easily overwhelmed by too much music coming at them too fast. So are your fellow musicians. Music with artfully placed breaks in the action is stronger and more artistically focused. It feels more connected with the core of creative expression, and it speaks with confidence and force.

Extended improvisations without such breaths do indeed have their place in jazz, as can been seen in the recordings of nearly every great jazz musician, but you should aim at making such moments the exception to the rule, rather than the rule itself.

Practice tactics and drills

1. Get your fingers moving.

If you're sitting down at your instrument and can't seem to get the creative juices flowing, try following your fingers. Play scales, play patterns, play melodies in various keys—play anything in your practice routine that will get the blood flowing through your veins. Your body is intimately connected to your soul; if your body is moving, your soul will move as well.

As always, be careful not to let your fingers play entirely mindlessly—for this would accomplish little more than solidifying bad habits—but you can and should allow them a certain amount of freedom as long as you stay emotionally and spiritually involved. And if you don't have the energy at a particular moment to stay actively involved or focused on your playing, opt for technical exercises or drills. In such cases mindless is OK, for your fingers will be learning discipline that is positive to your playing, rather than reinforcing bad habits.

2. *Practice slowly.*

Playing at reduced tempos exposes what we don't know; it reveals weaknesses in the internal logic and content of our lines, the holes in our vocabulary and the limitations on our ability to express ourselves. It allows us to focus much more of our energy on assuring that each note is played for a reason and contributes positively to the music. Many melodic phrases which basically pass mustard at a quick tempo—just playing in time and relatively close to the center of the beat, and ending with a nice ending phrase will usually be enough to sound "good"— but when they're slowed down we can really hear the weaknesses.

Playing at quicker tempos can be much easier than slower tempos. The beats are close to each other, so we always have a steady stream of pulses showing us the way and giving us confidence that we're solidly in the groove. At a slow tempo, we are forced more to use our own sense of time to fill the longer spaces between the beats. At 180 b.p.m., only one third of a second separates the beats, giving us signpost to let us know we're still on track. At 60 b.p.m., an entire second separates each beat from the next, forcing us to use our own sense of time to keep track of the rhythmic pulse.

Brisk tempos also makes us feel like we can play more melodically than we really can, for the bar for melody is naturally lower at fast tempos. The audience—ourselves included—cannot listen as effectively at quick tempos, making it much more difficult to discern which melodic lines are truly creative and which ones are essentially filler. If we slow down blistering jazz improvisations and listen to them at a lower speed, only the most inspired solos hold up under scrutiny. More often, blazing solos sound monotonous when heard or played at slower tempos. We see more filler material, more empty scales or patterns, or more instances of the fingers taking over, with little connection to true creativity.

I don't want to disparage burning solos in all cases, because it's not always essential for melodic improvisations to "hold up" under analytic scrutiny. There are much more important things at play, like such intangible qualities as inspiration and passion, as well as rhythmic excitement and emotional content. And sometimes playing fast, whether scales or patterns or memorized licks, is simply the most appropriate, artistically satisfying course of action. Played at breakneck tempos, even a major scale can sound hip—and that's OK—but it should be the exception rather than the rule

Playing slowly in practice imposes an important challenge, and challenge leads to progress. There's no place to hide when the music is slow, and if you can pull it off, the increased ability to focus on the notes you're playing, as well as the added vigor it will add to your melodic vocabulary, will be invaluable to your improvement.

3. Practice in every key.

Facility in all keys should be a fact of life. When we first start playing jazz, we naturally stick to the easy keys—C, F, Bb, and so forth. It's easier to stick to these keys, and when we learn new tunes they start sounding good much faster when we play them in familiar keys. But it doesn't take long until your weaknesses in other keys become painfully apparent.

Non musicians intrigued by the mystique of jazz often tell stories about old timers like Art Tatum or Charlie Parker, marveling at their ability play every tune in every key with no difference in quality. To an experienced jazz musician, such stories should not be cause for amazement. Such feats to be considered standard practice.

There are a number of advantages to playing in all keys, practically and creatively. On the practical level, you must simply be ready to perform in unconventional keys when required on a gig or at a jam session—and you will certainly be asked. Especially if you're playing with singers, you never know what key you'll be playing in.

Facility in all keys also allows you to better internalize the material you learn, as well as give you entirely new tools you can use in your improvisations. For instance, playing a particular piece of melodic lick in all keys can go a long way to better understanding the essence of that like. You are forced to conceptualize and internalize the structure of the lick—the intervals and rhythms that give it its character—and you develop a more intimate relationship with it. The same goes for the tunes you learn in all keys. You begin to recognize relationships between keys and between tunes that can improve your understanding of the music and improve your playing significantly.

4. Memorize.

If you're not memorizing repertoire and vocabulary, you're not advancing as much as you can. It's hard at first, but it opens endless doors when you get in the habit. Real books are severely frowned upon in professional situations. If you are to play jazz music, you are expected to know the tunes. And besides, sheet music is another crutch, and we want to eliminate crutches.

Everything but the creative spark should be eliminated from the equation—you should not need to "think about it"—while you're performing. Everything should be mastered so that in the moment of performance we can forget about it all and just make music. The tune should be so ingrained in you that you don't perform it, you reinvent it, and you use it as a springboard for new creations. There are many epiphanies to be had when the precomposed portion of the music is in the background of your mind, when you are free to expand on all of its shapes and crevices.

Don't just memorize tunes—memorize everything. And memorize it all as early in your learning process as possible. The faster it's learned the faster you can work on it more deeply and more efficiently. Forcing yourself to memorize something at the very beginning of the process can be tedious, but do it and do it with discipline. The extra effort in the early stages of the process will yield significant benefits, as it will allow every subsequent period of practicing after the memorization to be exponentially more useful.

When material is memorized in your mind, you can then make it memorized in your muscles. You program your fingers with the mechanical and intuitive feel of the material, making a natural, intimate part of your creative palette.

5. *Use a metronome.*

It seems like everyone thinks their time is perfect. If there's a rhythm issue in a performance, it always feels like it was the other guy who turned around the time, or the other guy who was rushing or dragging. Unless you're more self-aware than most, you feel like your beat is the right beat and anything different—faster, slower, whatever—is always wrong almost by definition. But everyone's time is flawed. And the more aware you can be of this fact the better your ability to make it better, and that's how you really better your rhythm. The best way to handle this problem is to use a metronome.

For a young musician, a metronome provides the central function of developing the most basic sense of pulse. It also prevents us from slipping in and out of time without knowing it. Try recordings yourself playing a tune you know well at a tempo you're comfortable with, then go back and listen to the recording. Snap or clap along with the recording and see if you added or subtracted beats, or if you paused entirely at some point, or stopped playing in time. Such things always happen more often than we think when we're early in our development.

It's particularly common to lose the time, or pause unknowingly, when we get to a part of a tune we don't know very well, or if a melodic line falls flat. But if you practice consistently with a metronome, you will be forced to keep a steady tempo, and hesitations or pauses you might otherwise disregard will be made clear. The metronome provides that objective standard, a reference point, which allows us to "check ourselves" to make sure we are not slipping into bad habits.

Without a metronome we all have the tendency to find certain tempos that just feel right, that feel like we're home. If someone counts off a particular tempo, you may believe you can easily pick it up and maintain it on your own throughout an entire performance with no variation. But more often, musicians tend to drift into one of a handful of distinct tempos that have been reinforced in practice sessions.

When you play tune at a medium swing tempo without a metronome, you may find yourself playing gravitating to the same tempo every time—140 b.p.m, for exam-

---

ple. In this case, you have internalized 140 b.p.m. subconsciously as your "go to" or "default" medium swing tempo. When someone snaps out a tempo at 130 b.p.m. and asks you to play unaccompanied, there's a good chance you'll find yourself speeding up to where you subconsciously feel medium swing should be. Or, if you're playing in band and someone snaps out 130 b.p.m. you may find yourself pushing to beat, in a subconscious effort to speed the band up to where it feels right to you.

Later, when your rhythmic sense becomes more fully developed, the function of the metronome can change somewhat. It can go from being a teacher—a disciplinarian leaning over your shoulder, letting you know when you make a mistake—to a crutch to lean on. Once you have a strong sense of tempo, and have reduced the habit of going in and out of time, you can get lulled into hearing the metronome as your beat, rather than providing your own, which makes you lazy. If this happen, and you can trust yourself enough not to unknowingly skip beats or push or drag unnecessarily, bypassing the metronome can be an effective tool to make sure you can internalize the real feel of the music—that you "provide the beat" yourself.

6. Practice with limitations.

There are no strict limitations on what you can or can't do in a jazz performance. You can play a whole solo with nothing but sixteenth notes. If you're a pianist, you can play the simple two-note guide tone voicings for every chorus of a tune. You can play the same note with the same rhythm for twenty minutes if you want to. All options are on the table. But when you're practicing, it's often important to impose limits on yourself.

When you've isolated an area of your playing you want to improve, try to limit yourself to practicing only that thing. If you want to learn how to play with space, do nothing but play with space. Set a timer, and see if you can do it for five minutes straight without losing your patience. If there's a melodic pattern you want to master, try playing it for five straight minutes without playing anything else. If you can't, try four minutes, or three—whatever you're capable of. Then you can increase form there.

Don't do it all the time, but dedicate a certain amount of your practice time to diligently placing limitations on what you can do. Command yourself to avoid a particular blues scale for five minutes while playing a particular tune. Or command yourself to play only the same blues on the same tune for five minutes, even if it doesn't really "work" theoretically. Play only high notes. Play only low notes. Play only soft notes. Play only loud notes.

The point is to place limitations and stick to them. This allows you to truly explore the techniques you want to master without allowing yourself to go off on unproductive tangents.

7. Play specific tunes for extended time.

They say Thelonious Monk would play the same tune all day when he practiced. It seemed like the strangest thing to me. I was in the misguided phase in which I was trying to memorize as many tunes as I could as fast as I could. I wanted prepared for jam sessions and gigs, and I frankly didn't have the patience to play the same tune for more than a few minutes at a time.

But when I found the discipline to play the same tunes repeatedly I was shocked and amazed at how much I discovered. I found more vocabulary that just came out of me—original stuff, stuff that came from inside me and not from any other source. It was good sounding stuff, creative and inspired.

There's something to be said about expanding your repertoire and maintaining a program of varied and diverse material. Versatility is indeed essential to playing music as a professional, especially jazz. With the dwindling opportunities to make actual money in this music, it is important for every musician to maximize their ability to find work—but please, take some time to really dig in to some tunes.

This rule doesn't even apply only to actual tunes; it works just as well with exercises, or even something as simple as a scale or mode. The point is to play the same thing over and over, reaching almost a meditative state. You get so comfortable that you can learn things at an instinctual level. Just like anything else you want to make second nature, the key is repetition. If you do something enough, it will become second nature, just like walking or talking or riding a bicycle. And when it's second nature, no longer requiring any conscious brainpower, you will gain insights that would otherwise be impossible.

8. Play in one key, or on one chord, for extended time.

Like extended practicing of repertoire, extended practice on specific keys (and modes) and chords is helpful in gaining intimacy with them, and making them a usable part of your musical vocabulary. Ask yourself what your weakest chord or scale types are your worsts, and spend some significant time practicing them. If it's a chord, compile all the melodic and harmonic options you have at your disposal to handle it—what scales can work on the chord, what chord alterations or substitutions are available, etc. If it's a key or a mode, compile all the options you have for handling it—chord voicings for comping, melodic patterns, chords that can be superimposed (e.g. diatonic chords), etc.

Also spend time just exploring the keys and chords. Turn on the metronome or use a play along recording and just keep playing, with discipline, and try to get in a creative trance that allows you to see new aspects of the chords and keys. Make them your friends.

9. "Shotgun" tunes to learn repertoire.

Ideally, we would only perform the repertoire we know intimately. The form would be second nature, the intricacies of the melodies would be like old friends, and there would be no distraction from focusing on pure creativity. After you've established yourself as an artist, it may be possible for you to only take the gigs you want to take, and only play the tunes you feel most comfortable playing. But until that happens, the importance of having an extensive repertoire cannot be ignored.

One way to efficiently expand the raw number of tunes under your grasp is a method called shotgunning. In this method, you line up a list of tunes you want to practice, and you bang them out swiftly and mechanically. Sometimes I will set a timer for one minute and force myself move on to the next tune when the timer goes off. I don't get to really dig in to tune, but I do get to go through the motions of playing the melody and chords. I think about the name of the tune, and because it happens so quickly, in some ways I replicate some of the factors that happen in real-world situations.

I believe that one of the best ways of increasing memory recall is repetition. If you are forced to recall something that you don't remember solidly, that very act of straining to remember it goes far in solidifying it in your memory. Think of it this way: I could either play a certain tune that I don't know very well for three minutes every week, or play it three times for one minute.

From the perspective of really exploring a tune to find its nuances, it would probably be better to spend more time each time I practice it. But for the tunes that won't be a central part of your repertoire, the ones you need to know just to be ready if it is called on a gig or jam session, the actual act of recalling it three times in a week goes farther for basic recall of large numbers of tunes.

By using this method, you will put yourself in an enviable position: on any given day, will have played every tune in your repertoire within the past week or so. You'll never have to sit there and think to yourself, "I know that tune, but I haven't played it forever." Each tune will be in your fingers, and for an expanded base of tunes, this will give you enviable versatility.

10. Transcribe.

Most jazz musicians (and teachers) liken learning to transcribe to learning to read. Once you can transcribe a solo—or a chord voicing, or a bassline—from a recording, you can decipher almost anything in recorded jazz, just like reading allows you access to the immeasurable knowledge contained in books. Transcribing allows you to pull out valuable material from the recordings that inspire you and the musicians you look up to. With diligent practice, the material gained through transcription can become a valuable component of your playing.

Transcribing is also an excellent way to connect deeply with the recorded music you love. It requires intense focus, and it demands a dedication of time, both of which are helpful in developing an intimate knowledge of the music you transcribe. Simply listening is not enough to fully decrypt the intricacies of a recording. You may think you really know a certain piano solo. But until you take the time to figure out every note and write it down (or memorize it straightaway), whatever understanding you get will be shallow and perfunctory.

The problem with transcribing has always been its difficulty. Especially with your first attempts, deciphering an entire solo can be a slow, tedious and frustrating experience. But it gets easier. And as you progress, the process will help you in all phases of your musicianship. A good rule of thumb is to start with the classic solos, and move out from there. Other musicians are familiar with the the great solos—it's a requisite of the job—and they will appreciate your work.

Approaches to transcription

There are quite a few approaches to transcribing; I will discuss two. The truly rigorous approach (and the most difficult) is to learn to sing the line you are attempting to transcribe without referring to your instrument. When you can competently and accurately sing it without accompaniment from the recording, the next step is to go to your instrument and figure out the actual note. If you have truly internalized the line in the first step, you will not need to reference the recording again when you are working with your instrument.

The intermediate step between listening to the music and picking it out on your instrument, forces you to truly absorb the music. You must develop your ear, and develop your tonal memory, or you won't be able to complete the process. As you advance, you begin to perceive each note as a note rather than a key on a piano or string on a guitar. Eventually, the goal is to be able to write down the musical content without any reference to the instrument at all (writing it straight to paper while listening). This is a virtuoso skill, one that takes years to develop, but this rigorous transcription method is the best way to acquire it.

However, the rigorous transcription method is also difficult and intimidating. And it is prone to frustrations so great that many musicians will forsake transcribing entirely. So, since I don't want you to give up on transcribing, I'll present you with the alternative, less rigorous approach, with hopes that as your ear develops sufficiently to allow you to move to the rigorous approach.

One such approach is to simply sit down at the instrument at the same time you have the music queued up on your music playing system (computers are best because you can easily repeat a particular section), and write down the notes as you figure them out. Transcription with the capability of slowing down recordings without changing the pitch can also be used to decipher particularly difficult passages. This method will allow you to pull whatever vocabulary you wish out of your favorite recordings, but it will not develop your ear or your tonal memory quite as quickly or effectively

Not everyone transcribes.

I don't want to tell you not to transcribe; that would be absurd. Transcription is one of the central aspects of the cultural of practicing and learning jazz, so I can't go against that. I am myself a strong proponent of transcription; I've done tons of it, and I'll keep doing tons of it; and every time I do it I feel a strong sense of satisfaction and achievement. I feel closer to the music I love, and I feel more in informed, more in touch, and more authentic as a musician. Most importantly, it makes me a better player.

But, all that said, it is not a requirement. Mulgrew Miller never did, not once (he told me himself). No one could argue that Miller is not connected deeply with the tradition of jazz. His melodies are well informed by the bebop tradition of Charlie Parker and Dizzy Gillespie, and his harmonies reveal deep understanding of everything from Oscar Peterson to Red Garland to Bill Evans to Herbie Hancock. His rhythmic feel one of the most swinging and genuine in jazz today. But Mulgrew never transcribed.

I've often wondered how Mulgrew could have done. Everything about his playing is so delightfully authentic. But it is difficult to comprehend how he could absorb the vocabulary if he didn't "figure it out" then learn it through practice. The best answer I can come up with—and it's probably far from the truth—is that Mulgrew either has the uncanny ability to precisely know what musicians are playing when they're playing it (or when he's hearing them on a record). Or maybe with many repeated listenings, or with a freakish memory, he can simply recall the real details of the performance much more effectively than the average musician. Either way, we must be careful not to let Mulgrew's experience teach us that simple listening is enough. We have to take it seriously and in a focused manner—regardless of if we transcribe or not.

Listening to music can like looking at a blurry picture. Or a clear picture from far away. It's just hard to see the tiny details. But if we were to copy a work of art just by looking at it from a distance, any casual observer could walk up to our reproduction and easily observe that the details simply aren't there. From far away it looks like the real thing, but it just doesn't look right under the scrutiny of anything more than a perfunctory glance more that perfunctory glance—even if you can't quite put your finger on it. Transcription can lead to a clear picture and an authentic assimilation and reinvention of the jazz that touches you.

11. Don't play every note or chord.

It's not always necessary, or even advisable, to play all the chords in a tune. It's certainly not advisable to play every note in a scale or key. In fact, harmonically simplifying a tune, especially during improvised sections, can be an excellent way to open up a performance. In your practicing, dedicate some time to specifically removing information from the tunes you play.

Set a timer—not for too long, say 10 minutes—and promise yourself to do nothing but simplify the tune you're working on. Leave out any chords that aren't necessary. Play through the melody a few times and pare down any unnecessary notes. Try choosing just one note per measure to represent the melody, and then try to find one note that works for two chords. Do the same thing with chords. Keep going until you can simplify an entire tune to its most fundamental core. Become intimate with this core. This will allow you more freedom to improvise while keeping you grounded in the composition.

12. Generalize the chords.

Especially in the more inspired, freer moments of an improvisation, simplifying a chord progression to its bare bones can give a simple but honest base on which extraordinary explorations can be built. Everybody does it, and if you're not used to it, you can often be confused by what you hear in recordings and on the bandstand. In fact, it's quite rare that a band sticks to the actual chords in a performance.

This ability is particularly important when playing tunes with many acceptable variations. Tunes that can be easily simplified, such as those based on I-iv-ii-V progressions or iii-vi-ii-V—which are essentially the same thing—are often thought of as big fat I chords. Why can we do this? Because despite the four chords, both progressions are just turnarounds to get back to the tonic.

To prove it, just play the major blues scale over either progression—it sounds perfect. Also, check out recordings of tunes with these progressions—any rhythm changes tune, Have You Met Miss Jones, etc.—and you'll find that the greatest musicians play much more of the generalized progression, playing around with the I chord, than marking out each individual chord. Your exclusive goal should not be to simplify in your playing, but it is an important tool to have in your toolbox that can provide freedom, variety, and contrast in your playing.

13. Take advantage of technology.

Learn how to use notation software—or at least to write down musical notation really fast. There's nothing more frustrating than having an amazing idea in your mind or in your fingers and be forced to either forget it or stop the creative process so much to sit down and take ten minutes to write it on paper. By the time you're done writing it down, you might not want to go back to the instrument, or you may not be feeling creative. And you will most certainly have an incredibly difficult time getting back to the same creative place you were in when you decided to take the break from creativity and start tediously scribbling on paper or clicking at the computer. But if you're fast, then everything changes. The goal is to eliminate anything that may stop you from easily getting your work done.

The Skills Checklist

1. The blues.

In the dominion of jazz repertoire, the blues reigns supreme. I doubt there is much more I can say here than you already know, so I'll be brief. Even if you have no designs of being a great blues player, and even if you want to avoid the entire mainstream, traditional jazz scene, it is essential to have familiarity with the blues. Every key, every tempo. Live it. Learn it. No exceptions.

Know the traditional chord changes as well as the so-called "jazz blues" changes (with the added ii-V-I progressions). You should also be prepared with common substitutions, turnarounds, introductions, and endings. Know plenty of melodies too. Just because the chords progressions are essentially the same in almost all blues tunes, don't get caught off guard by not knowing the melodies themselves.

Extensive practice of the blues will improve your playing in almost all areas of jazz performance and improvised music in general. Because of the relatively static nature of the blues (4 bars on the I chord, 4 bars on the IV chord, and so on), playing the blues will provide you with invaluable skills in telling and interesting story with relatively static harmonic framework. The vocabulary you practice, as well as the vocabulary you figure out through your own experimentation in the blues, can provide a central

But please don't get trapped, like so many jazz musicians, into thinking that improvising over the blues is no more than noodling around with blues scales. This approach is popular because it's easy and the results are fast and sounds reasonably good. For beginners this may seem sufficient, but a serious jazz musician must attack the blues with vigor and diligence.

2. *Rhythm Changes.*

Rhythm changes—the class of chord progressions derived from the harmony of Gershwin's "I Got Rhythm"—are second only to the blues in the canon of jazz repertory orthodoxy. Like the blues, rhythm changes are omnipresent at jam sessions and professional gigs, and being able to manipulate them adroitly is an art in itself.

Practicing rhythm changes is a great way to work on some of the most common and important harmonic gestures and techniques in jazz. It's got plenty of ii-V-I's, and plenty of common modulations (from the I to the IV and back in the A section). The bridge section includes dominant chords for two measures a piece—often a challenge for younger musicians—as well as ample opportunity to experiment substitutions. Rhythm changes also provides the opportunity to experiment with simple riffs—blues-based or otherwise—played over multiple chords.

Much can also be learned from playing rhythm changes at varying tempos. At burning tempos, explicitly outlining each chord of the A section—only two beats each—can be exceedingly difficult. The ability to clearly define the chords as they pass by at breakneck speeds is an important skill to possess, and you will gain much by practicing it, but it is not employed as often as you might think.

As you will see with extended practice and listening, it's not common outline every chord of rhythm changes at fast tempos. More often, musicians generalize the harmony considerably. A sections are simplified such that the basic turn arounds are either not played or played less consistently. Some take a quasi-modal approach. Even more often, most of the A section becomes a playground for blues licks—and they sound good.

At slower tempos, outlining the specific harmony—as well as contributing your own harmonic substitutions—is much more important. It becomes more beneficial to add harmony at these tempos rather than take it away, though with practice, a generalized approach in the hands of a master can be transcendentally inspired. Extensive, repeated practice of rhythm changes at various tempos will reveal these intricacies to you.

When you learn new vocabulary, applying it to rhythm changes can often be a beneficial first step toward working it into your usable, performance vocabulary. If you're working on a new ii-V-I lick, for instance, look for all the opportunities in rhythm changes to apply it and practice them in context. The same goes for simple blues licks or any other tidbit of vocabulary you're working on.

Also, write out a few solos for rhythm changes; they'll come in handy, giving you something to vary and abstract in your improvisations. The same goes with voicings and rhythmic vocabulary. Make rhythm changes a regular part of your practice routine and you will cover a great deal of techniques and vocabulary central to the core of jazz performance.

3. *Repertoire*

Just because you're an improviser, doesn't mean you don't need a repertoire of performance-ready compositions. You may find strict memorization of jazz standards trivial, but without a considerable repertoire, you will find that playing with other musicians is an exceedingly difficult task. There are a surprising number of jazz musicians that fall into this category, however. Almost every time you get together with a group of musicians, finding a common batch of tunes to play together can be a chore—especially with younger musicians. So do yourself a favor and never let something as simple as not knowing the tune stop you from what could be a meaningful music experience.

Separate the tunes that comprise your principal creative repertoire—the ones you know the best and consider the best vehicles for your creativity—from the tunes you know just well enough to get by. Ideally, your entire repertoire should fall into the first category, but practical considerations make this impossible. Until you can gain the years of real-world experience that will allow you to be truly comfortable with vast numbers of tunes, select a smaller number—say 20 or 30—to be your main artistic repertoire, while steadily bulking up your secondary, "competent" list.

Know how you're going to start each tune, and know how to finish it. If you're a pianist, be ready to set up an introduction to each tune if needed, and know how you're going to lead the band to an ending. If you're going to tag an ending, know which bars will be tagged. If you know it's a tune that is played differently by different people ("Round Midnight," for instance, has a number of distinct but accepted sets of chord changes used in common practice), know all the versions. And be ready to communicate with the other people you're playing with so you're on the same page. See the appendices for categorized lists of suggested tunes, as well as my thoughts on the tunes you should learn first and practice the most.

4. Scales.

Most musicians dread the notion of practicing scales. They are considered tedious and boring. In a commendable ruse to avoid scales, many jazz musicians claiming that they lead to "overly technical" or "mechanical" playing, that they have no soul. Though over reliance on scales can certainly lead to vapid, empty improvisations—which should be avoided at all costs—the simple fact is that they are a necessary component of jazz.

Without an understanding the subtleties of scale theory, and a facility in maneuvering through them in performance, significant dimensions will be lost in your improvisations. Extensive practice with scales, which should include straight "running up and down" the scale in various rhythms as well as various patterns and drills, will allow you to have a "home base" in your improvisations. Every standard tune progresses through various chord changes, providing a harmonic framework for both the tune itself and the improvisations based on it. But the harmonic framework can also be thought of in terms of tonal centers, or keys. Knowing what tonal center you're in, using scales as your reference point, is an important part of exploring the very core of a tune.

5. *Modal jazz.*

Modal jazz improvisation foregoes the typical formula of jazz harmony, replacing the usual series of changing chords with a much more static harmony grounded in modes. One advantage to playing modal jazz is that the static nature of the harmony allows for you to think less about what chord is coming next and more about your artistic ideas. A disadvantage is that the lack of harmonic variety can make modal playing rather dull, unless you add harmonic, rhythmic, or melodic interest yourself.

Familiarize yourself with the important modes, starting with the those based on the major scale. The Dorian mode (based on the second degree of the Major scale, or the ii-minor chord) and the Mixolydian mode are the most commonly used modes, so you should be comfortable playing them for extended periods. Also essential is the altered scale, which is the common name for the seventh mode of the melodic minor scale. It is one of the best ways to handle altered dominant chords. If you have these three modes mastered, you're in good shape. See the appendices for strategies on mastering these modes, as well as suggestions for further modal study.

6. *Know the common harmonic gestures.*

In the traditional jazz idiom, almost all standard repertoire consists of reshuffled combinations of common harmonic combinations, which I call "harmonic gestures." A ii-V-I progression is what I would call a harmonic gesture. It's more than a chord, but less than a whole tune.

There can also be classes and subclasses of harmonic gestures. Within the ii-V-I class, for instance, ii-V progressions that proceed to the relative minor of a particular tonic represents a more specific subclass. With 10 or 15 of of the most common harmonic gestures under your belt, you can probably form almost all jazz standards in the jazz canon.

Knowing these common gestures, and being easily capable of recognizing them, allows you to more easily break down compositions into their distinct parts. Doing this allows you to better understand the structure of the tune, and it allows you to memorize it more easily. Rather than remembering every chord, you are only responsible for a remembering a few gestures.

You will also be better positioned to target your practicing of vocabulary. Start thinking about melodic and harmonic vocabulary in terms of how it applies to specific harmonic gestures, then be ready when you see those gestures in tunes to employ this vocabulary.

Recognize similarities between tunes, based on harmonic gestures they share. For example, how many tunes contain and A section (or A sections) that basically stay in the tonic of the tune before proceeding to a bridge on the IV? If you haven't already start noticing, take some time to break down some tunes, looking at them from a big picture perspective, and see if you can make a list of tunes that follow this formula. It won't be difficult.

Review common harmonic gestures listed in the appendices, then start looking for gestures you see popping up repetitively in your practicing and performing. Start thinking of the tunes you're learning, and the tunes you already know, in terms of these gestures. And when you listen to music, especially music you don't know very well, try to listen for these gestures.

If you can't figure out all the chords when you're listening to an unfamiliar tune, perhaps you can make out a general gesture, like a move to the IV chord on the bridge. Keep it up and you will be able to more easily pick out the common gestures in what you hear and what you read on the page.

7. Blues licks.

8. Know how to reharmonize.

Reharmonizing is not just for pianists. Every jazz musician should know how to manipulate, superimpose, and otherwise alter the harmonic framework of the compositions in their repertoire. Almost no one plays a tune as it's written. Your reharmonization toolkit should consist of both preconceived reharmonizations of the tunes in your repertoire you know best and a collection of "tricks" you can apply in certain situations on the fly, when you're playing either tunes you don't know well or tunes you're playing for the first time.

There area an awful of lot of harmonic tricks that have become common practice in jazz, and unfortunately you'll have to know almost all of them. See the appendices of this book for advice on where to start your exploration of reharmonizations.

9. Diatonic patterns

Diatonic patterns are repetitive segments of melodic material that can be manipulated around a particular scale or mode. Moving up and down a scale arpeggiating each diatonic chord could be an example of a diatonic pattern.

It's easy to go overboard with such patterns, so use them with care, but make sure to have a few up your sleeve. They can help you out of many jams, and they provide an excellent way to connect other melodic ideas, as well as give you a solid melodic base to fall back on in difficult situations. With extensive practice, these patterns can also allow you to find more original and personal bits of melodic vocabulary you can call your own.

When learning a pattern, make sure you can play it on all the common scales and modes, and make sure you can seamlessly switch between modes without disturbing the pattern. In other words, practice playing a pattern through entire progressions, changing the scale or mode as necessary without changing the pattern.

For instance, for a ii-V-I progression in which you'd like to play the altered dominant scale for the V chord, try to maintain a consistent pattern throughout the progression, starting Dorian mode of the ii chord, progressing to the altered dominant scale of the V chord, then proceed to the Ionian (Major) scale of the I chord (which is composed of the same pitch classes as the Dorian mode of the ii chord). Work each pattern you learn through various progressions of this type—including entire tunes—in all keys. See the appendices of this book and the companion website for more examples and strategies.

10. Improvising on vamps.

Vamps are short, cyclic harmonic progressions or rhythmic ostinatos that are repeatedly indefinitely, usually until a cue is given to stop or move on to the next section. They can vary in length from one to a few measures.

Common vamps are the iii-VI-ii-V progression or its close relatives or a pedal point on the V chord of the tune. Vamps are often used to start and end tunes.

In practice sessions, repeat the vamps you want to master extensively, first slowly, exploring the insides and outsides of the chords or grooves, then at full speed. Make sure while you're doing this to keep track of your counting. Try to feel what four measures of a vamp feels like, or eight measures. It's important to develop this sense, for it makes communication with your fellow band members easier and music making more effective and meaningful.

11. Counting off.

If you are a leader, counting off a tune is one of the most important moments in a tune, so you should take it seriously. If you're playing in style with swing eighth notes, standard practice is to snap your fingers on beats two and four for a few seconds to give the band a feel for the tempo, then to quietly say or mouth a count off ("1-2-3-4") to get the band started. It is an important mark of a good leader and a strong musician to count off effectively. Make sure when your snapping your fingers not to vary the tempo, unless you need to.

Try to avoid changing the tempo after you've started snapping, even if you haven't yet started the count off. Speeding up and slowing down while snapping can give the band members mixed messages. If you're not confident you can start snapping at the right tempo on your first snap, try silently getting yourself into the rhythmic feel of the piece, perhaps by humming the melody to yourself. It's easy to feel that a certain tempo is appropriate while you're just snapping it, only to find out when the melody comes in that it's far too fast or slow. Thinking of or humming the melody to yourself before you start snapping can help you avoid this situation. On difficult or unfamiliar tunes, singing a few bars of the melody to the band can be an effective way bring to give the group a collective

Also beware of rhythmic sloppiness in the moments immediately before and after you start playing. Inexperienced jazz musicians often snap at a nice, steady pace, only to speed up or slow down when the actual count off begins. Or they will count off a certain tempo only to immediately speed up on the first downbeat of the tune. Root out any similar tendencies of your own and eliminate them.

12. Handling train wrecks.

Losing the form is inevitable. Especially with less experienced players, a band will often get hopelessly lost, twisted, and turned around. When it happens to more than one or two band members, the performance can get very ugly very quickly. It's frustrating—and often embarrassing—but you must know how to handle such situations when they arise.

Your first reaction should be to open your ears, like putting up an antenna, and focus all your attention on the search for clues as to where you are in the form. Everyone in the band should do the same. Hopefully, one or more members of the band will still know where they are, and you can listen for harmonic or rhythmic signals from them that can help you situation yourself. If they haven't realized you're lost, establishing eye contact will usually do the trick, and they should respond by playing particularly clearly or making explicit gestures that can serve as guides.

It also makes sense to look to the rhythm section for guidance. Unless you're the leader of the group, and you have exceptional skills in leading a band out of a train wreck, it's likely that the rhythm section can do a better job leading the way. If the bassist and the drummer are on the same page, it will be easy to dig out of trouble. If they are not paying attention, it's best to follow them, if they are playing clearly enough to make it possible, because it's exceptionally difficult to make a tune feel right if the bass player is a measure or two off. It's just in the nature of the instrument.

In the worst-case scenario, someone may have to raise their hand, count out four beats and call out which section or measure to start on. Something like "**1**, **2**, **Le**-tter, **A**," where the bold, underlined letters and numbers represent strong beats. This would direct everyone to play at letter A at the end of the four beats. You could also call out something like "top of the form," then pause to make sure everyone understands. When it's clear everyone is on the same page, you can then count out four beats to bring it all together. Such actions are embarrassing, since they make it perfectly clear to the audience that something went unusually wrong, and should be considered a last resort.

It doesn't matter if measures are ultimately skipped or added, as long as everyone eventually finds their way to the same chord at the same time. And it doesn't matter who's right or who's wrong, or who may have caused the train wreck in the first place. Don't be stubborn if you have to follow the rest of the band to another part of the form, even if you have absolute confidence that kept the form perfectly. As in all group situations, the good of the band eclipses the good of the individual.

13. Simplify the form.

Sometimes the goal is to add chords to the harmonic rhythm, introducing your own substitutions to heighten the harmonic complexity and interest of the composition. On the other hand, sometimes it's far more advantageous to leave chords out. Be ready to exploit these differences, which can add valuable variety and interest to your playing.

For Pianists

1. Know your voicings.

Every functional jazz pianist must be prepared to play every chord type in every key without hesitation. This includes both left hand voicings, to accompany one's right hand when soloing) and two hand voicings, to accompany others or during heads. As the pianist progresses it will be come important to move beyond the restrictions of simply playing various chord voicings to comp—such as more "orchestral" or "pianistic" techniques—but a well-prepared and rehearsed arsenal of interesting and colorful voicings for each chord will go miles to establish the essential vocabulary of a creative jazz pianist.

Guide tone-only voicings

Two Note Voicings
          a) play with your thumbs
A and B Voicings (3rd on bottom vs. 7th on bottom)

I will adopt the practice of Andy Leverne to describe two very standard ways to look at chord voicings: A and B voicings. Simply, this system is meant to provide a simple way to differentiate voicings in which the 3rd is the bottom guide tone and in which the 7th is the bottom guide tone. Since we are raising the guide tones to a preeminent position in our system of harmony, it makes sense for us to base our vocabulary for talking about harmony around these essential elements.

So, here's the rule:

Let's get the whole notion of what a two-note voicing is. What two-note voicings are: the 3rd and 7th of each chord. The 3rd and 7th are the "colorful" parts of the chord, the parts that actually define the chord variety. What's left over? The root and the 5th. Though these notes are undoubtedly important in their way, the do nothing to define chord color. Of course the root decides which actual chord or "key" the chord variety is attached to, but this is unnecessary; our ear naturally extrapolates this information, and in almost all situations in which these voicings are used we are also playing with a bass player, which takes care of the root.

The fifth is also generally considered unnecessary. Going back to our general desire for every not to serve a purpose, the fifth doesn't do much. Yes, there are times it serves a rather important purpose—when you simply need to "thicken" a voicing, mostly for purposes of adding power—but such uses come later. For now, let's avoid the fifth (especially in lower registers).

But we are more interested in building our vocabulary "from the bottom up," starting with building blocks that we need, and that we can control, and moving toward "adding" in extra pieces when we feel they can add a new nuance to our playing, or a new color.

Just listen to Wynton Kelly comping for his own solos. Even when comping for others you sometimes here him sticking to simple two note voicings. He certainly has the full physical capacity to use both hands, and still some of the crispest, most powerful two-hand voicings in the jazz canon, so why do he and so many others do it? Because it sounds good, and it's the right thing to do. In short, it is the best way to contribute positively to the music.

Two note voicings are simply the most efficient, "cost-effective" way to express the true sound of a chord without sacrificing any of the true character of the harmony. This voicing has the additional advantage of allowing for almost virtually infinite additions and adaptations.

Once you have mastery of the two-note voicing, then you can wrap your mind around everything else. And when you're still grappling with everything else—which will probably be your whole life—you can always have the confidence that you still have the guide tone trick in your back pocket.

Figure: One of each
--note on range
depending on key, A and B will be very favorable.
Figure: A+B voicings in all keys, but only the ones that make the most sense in terms of range

–Three note
–Four note

NOTE: about the range of the voicings.

This one has become surprisingly controversial recently—and for good reason (in my humble opinion). Yes, the classic jazz standards are masterpieces. They have stood the test of time and they are infinite sources of inspiration. And they already have such a body of performances and recordings that they provide the ideal "common ground" for many jazz conversations between musicians.

But at the same time, they are very old. And I must recognize here that there is a whole world of jazz that can be learned and performed without them. I just remember a conversation I had recently with an absolutely first-rate NYC musician, who's getting oodles of work these days (and good work too). "I can't remember the last time I played All the Things you are." There are extraordinary openings these days in the world of improvised music, and some of them

The argument can be made that these new opportunities are not jazz, and the argument holds water. In my definition many of these new places are still called jazz— and, incidentally, virtually all the musicians that play these styles are extraordinarily well-versed in playing traditional and nontraditional jazz over the standard repertory—and.....

But for the sake of this book—and for the sake of the generally accepted view of jazz—the standard repertory is essential. After all, all the voicings and rhythms discussed in these pages refers to a certain subset of music—a certain musical vocabulary, even language—and the repertory is an integral part to that system.

The standard repertory should be referenced constantly in your practicing.

As a rule, make a point of practicing everything you do, every piece of melodic, harmonic or rhythmic vocabulary, in the context of a tune or portion of a tune. Don't just play major chords an hour, then minor chords for an hour, and so on and so on. Rather, put the vocabulary you're working on into the context of a tune.

Luckily, standards are generally very similar to each other.

2. Basslines.

The ability to play adequate basslines has been lost to many modern piano players. Well, in my opinion it's been lost for a very long time. Even in the classic era of jazz piano only the special exception pianist could really do it. In addition the extraordinary practical benefits of being able to play swinging, powerful basslines—like when you need to accompany a sax player or vocalist without a bass player or drummer—there are also extremely useful benefits to solo piano playing, and to increasing our mastery of the instrument overall.

Jazz piano has really ignored the left hand to a large extent. Even those who pay lip service to the left hand often don't really let it out of its shell, keeping it within the traditional role of playing chunky chords, relatively static, while the right hand plays single note melodies. This style really works, as it has been developed over many decades and has entered many interesting avenues of music. But it's just too limited in my view.

At the very least, the right thing to do is to increase your awareness of what your left hand is doing. Make it a real voice and pay attention to that voice. You can play chords, but when you conceptually decide to it the respect it deserves as an actual musical voice, you can make the notes in the chords you play sing, and that will naturally come out in your playing.

I am of the opinion, however, that there are just so many more places to go with the left hand that it would an absolute shame to leave it like this. The left hand has just as many fingers as the right hand, and it has the same physical capacity as the right. It just sadly lack the training in most pianists.

Basslines are a good way to gain a little independence. It's not the most original thing in the world, but as a part of a general strategy to gain independence, it works well. You can't play a good bassline while maintaining strong playing with your right hand without a good amount of discipline and independence. And after such independence can be attained, the path toward further avenues to explore becomes clear in ways that I couldn't explain here.

See the appendix of this book for some simple basslines to drill. Unfortunately, strong left hand lines can only be mastered with excessive repetitions. They must be repeated many times before they are second nature and it is most muscle memory that makes your left hand move.

Most people believe that the most a person can truly pay attention to is two independent lines at once. That doesn't mean that we can't enjoy more than two over the course of a piece of music or a section of a piece of music. It's just that our brain can very quickly shift its focus from one place to another, and it also has the uncanny ability to "fill in the gaps" of what we don't physically hear but it shows up in our mind as what we think is the sensation of sound.

On Listening

1. Separate "work listening" from "pleasure listening."

Listening to music in the background while you're doing the dishes or folding the laundry is not the same as listening in a focused state, free of distractions. Listening for pure enjoyment, even if your focus is high, is also different from listening for the purposes of work. All of these types of listening are important and beneficial, but keep an awareness of what kind of listening you do on a regular basis. If upon careful reflection you find that the majority of your listening is background listening, work more active listening into your daily routine.

Listening is an exceedingly personal experience, so you must find your own way to handle it. But I encourage you to take it seriously, as something worthy of significant planning and goal setting. Just like the goals you set for your playing, you should set goals for your listening, and you should make appropriate plans to attain them.

2. *Keep a listening notebook.*

It doesn't have to be fancy, and it certainly doesn't have to be comprehensive, but the act of writing down notes on your listening will greatly enrich the experience.

Early in my development as a musician and listener, I remember obsessively listening to the same handful of albums for weeks and months at a time. I certainly learned from this listening, but at one point I had a surprising realization about how much I was missing. Whenever I had to talk about the music to anyone else, some of the simplest things escaped me. The simplest question, like "what are your favorite songs" would sometimes give me trouble.

The way I had listened was completely divorced from knowing the names of the songs. I never looked at the names, and I barely looked at the track numbers on the CD player, so I had very little connection between what I was hearing and what the songs were I was listening to.

Rather than know my favorite tracks, I would just play albums from beginning to end, listening for basic enjoyment until my favorite moments in the recordings arrived, when I would pay special attention and just be happy. If I wanted to extract vocabulary out of these moments in a practical, usable way, it was much more difficult, because I was rarely thinking about the context in which these moments appeared.

To this day, I have to make a specific, concerted effort to sit down and listen to music so that I am fully aware of the full context of the individual songs. It's far to easy to just put on an album and just listen to it beginning to end without pausing or thinking about the individual compositions.

The best way to receive the full benefits of deep listening is to keep a journal. It forces you to "check in" with your analytical side and prevents you from zoning out too much. A certain amount of brainless pleasure listening is important, and there's no reason to take this out of your life, but be sure to spend time digging deeply and methodically into the recordings you want to learn from. If you are passive in your listening, you are very likely missing out on quite a bit of useful stuff.

Another experience that pushed me into the idea of a listening journal was in wine tasting. When you go to a good wine tasting,

I once took a wine tasting class. We would taste about 5-8 wines per class, and at the beginning of every class I felt, "I'll won't forget these wines. There are only 5 of them, and besides, I only need to know about the ones I like." I felt that as soon as I tasted the wines I would have a good understanding of the taste and this understanding would be recorded in my mind. Then, the next time I tasted the same varietal or a wine from the same region, I would be able to recall the information and be able to make comparisons in my mind, and therefore increasing the depth of my understanding.

It didn't take me long to understand the professor's insistence on taking notes about the wines. By answering just a handful of questions, it was quite easy to scribble down enough notes to better conceptualize the sensations of drinking the wine and record it in a way that would make it more difficult to forget.

The questions were simple. You'd be asked to rate the wine on a scale of one to ten, or place it on a scale of dry versus sweet. They were easy questions, but they forced to me to put at least a little thought into me answers, and and by placing my thoughts into categories, as simple as they were, I deepened my understanding of the wine.

I firmly believe the act of writing something down greatly aids the creation of associations and categories in our minds that enhance our ability to understand and memorize. And remembering is a big part of the game. It's also the act of going back and reminding yourself of something after you've forgotten it. There's nothing better for forming a real, authentic memory.

There is only a finite amount of listening time available in one's life, so we should all be careful with how we use our time. We mustn't lose our listening for pure pleasure, free from any intellectual thought or analysis. But we must also use our conscious, intellectual mind to guide our listening habits. This allows our allowing our listening to be inspiring and pleasurable, while at the same time vastly improving the effectiveness of our development.

The journal is key for this. After you have a few entries, especially if they are thoughtful and concise, you can glance over tens or even hundreds of tunes in just a few page flips. And with this quick review, you can easily make a plan for the stuff you really want to listen to—the recordings you want to focus on and study at a higher level.

You also want to take more notes on the moments in the recordings you like the most. These notes don't need to be extensive, but if you have a list of tunes that you're going to focus on for a week, and you love the piano solo on one of them—or even just a measure or two of the piano solo—write it down! If you write it down, even once, from that moment on it will always be "that piano solo that I wrote down the other day" instead of just a few moments of music that make you happy whenever it comes up on your CD player of iPod. That solo, or those solos, or those moments, or those tunes will be come "things" that live and grow, and because they were written down they will be placed in a category within your mind, even in your subconscious, and they will develop into much stronger memories. This is the key to effective listening.

Thoughts on music journals and listening playlists

Most of the time when I listen to music I play my favorite albums from beginning to end. There's a lot of beauty to this method of listening, especially if you're listening to a well-crafted album on which the artist spent significant effort planning as a cohesive statement overall, but it's also very easy not to get the most out of it.

If it's an album you truly love, and you have an unusual ability to concentrate, truly immersed in every aspect of the music, this kind of listening might be enough. You probably don't need any pointers at all because you have developed such a strong ability to listen that you can just learn straight from the recordings without spending extensive meticulous effort on breaking it down.

But most people, whether they know it or not, even musicians, need an extra push to really get the most out of the music. And I think breaking up albums is a great way to do this. When you listen to an album beginning to end, it's too easy to zone out. You hear the stuff you love and really pay attention to that. Then the first song you don't love you zone out a little bit. Then, a little bit down the road something might come up that could be truly engaging and beautiful but it might not necessarily have the energy or excitement to snap you out of your

That's another reason I strongly support the idea of keeping a listening journal. Just the action of jotting down a few words—just take 10 seconds!—for every track as you are listening to an album makes you more engaged. You have to listen at least once, for at least part of the song, to make a somewhat intelligent observation to record in your journal. You can't zone out the whole time. At least one moment for each track you are actually listening to it.

Even better, you will know which tracks, if any, you are going to put on your "priority playlist." The stuff that will be your "default" listening for the day, or the week, or the month. I often have a lot of trouble deciding what to listen to. There's just so much music to chose from, and so much of it is good, that sometimes I even avoid sticking my earphones in my ears because I subconsciously know that it's going to be a tough decision. It's not that I fear to start listening, but it's so much easier to just slip into laziness or distraction.

Without someone telling you to *listen now*, sometimes it's easier to just sit at the piano and noodle around. Or pick up a book and start reading. Any little inconvenience can make it harder for you to start doing something, like listening, but once you start you can't stop. So the key is to get you started.

If you always have a priority playlist, and you keep it fresh by reviewing it often—like every week—you will always have something that you will both enjoy to listen to and will get you something that will really help in whatever you are working on practice wise during that time.

Advanced Material and Concepts

1. Exploring the beat: ahead of, behind, and in the middle of the beat. Make your rhythm dance.

As Mulgrew Miller repeatedly told me and his other students, one must really make sure that whatever he or is doing stands up to snuff by itself. Specifically, if one's feel and rhythm is right on and "dances"—to use another Mulgrew favorite—then you will be really contributing to the music.

One way I've found to make sure you yourself have the "dance" in your playing—and Mulgrew did this too—is to try to put it into the music without a metronome. After years of practice, we can actually start feeling the pop of the metronome as swinging itself.

To put this to the test, try getting into a real groove, with your metronome set to beats 2 and 4, as usual. After a few minutes, have a friend turn off the metronome at an unexpected time. You'll go from being as comfortable as can be to feeling like you don't have any ground to stand on. Here you will discover that you really need to have your internal rhythm so solid that your time is as good when the metronome is on as when it is.

Making your rhythm dance is something an advanced concept. Though it is never to early to make such a thing a primary goal, the kind of subtle concept I'm referring to here requires extensive experience and study to even discern, so I believe it's more important to take care of the fundamentals of rhythm to start.

It is also nice to take advantage of other kinds of modern technology, especially with the advent of smart phones and tablets and apps that run on them. Apps on these devices, as well as some of the more fancy metronomes, can take the role of the "friend" I mentioned before

2. *Odd Meters.*

3. *Polyrhythms*

4. *Modern, difficult chord changes.*

(Monk, Wayne, Herbie).

5. *Even more difficult chord changes (a la David Binney).*

6. *Free Playing.*

Appendices

Further Reading/Reference

The Jazz Piano Book by Mark Levine. Sher Music.

The Jazz Theory Book by Mark Levine. Sher Music.

This book is even more helpful than Levine's Jazz Piano book, even for the pianist. These first two books are pretty much the standard-bearers of jazz books. They are comprehensive, well researched and balanced. Nearly everything in them is valuable, and they should never be far from the musician's easy reach. There are many transcriptions and nearly all musical examples are complete with specific references to particular musicians and recordings. I have gained extensively from these resources, and I'd like to consider my little book to be something of a "little brother" to these volumes—the distilled, easy to read, easy to carry around version, nothing but the essentials and little bit of inspiration along with the technical advice. You should own both of these books. In fact, if you own these two books, there isn't much need of any more, unless you want to get quite specific. But rest assured, there are plenty of pages in there, and all of them have gold, so don't miss a thing.

The Primacy of the Ear. Ran Blake. 2010 Third Stream Associates. Available at Lulu.com and Amazon.com, among others.

This book is readable and useful. Ran has been an important influence on my development as a musician. His ideas are rigorous, unique, and absolutely worth a very close look and even an intense period of study. This book outlines pretty much his entire philosophy of music, which centers on his unique style of ear training.

There's nobody better at truly finding a way to find a unique voice and transcend the confines of genre or style (though he's intensely aware of style). He's an interesting man and this is an interesting book. You might, like me, end up coming back to the book time and time again either for inspiration or for some pointers on how to whip your ears into shape. Every time I pick it up I feel like a more serious and better musician. I couldn't recommend this book more.

Berliner Jazz Book.

Online Resources

Bert Ligon site

Appendix I: Tips on keeping a journal

You can really see your progress.
It's important to keep yourself honest in your work.

The central aspects of a journal for me are as follows:
Practice routine, ready to be checked off.
List of goals, short term and long term.
Repertoire lists.
Vocabulary.

Appendix II: Great tunes to practice and why

Bye Bye Blackbird

Everyone knows this tune. It's also one of the best tunes to practice playing over I chords for extended times. At the very beginning of an improver's career, the easiest thing in the world is to just blow over one chord jams. It's easy because you don't have to think too much about changing harmony and you can really just wailed on the same little group of notes and have a fair amount of control over what you're doing. But as you progress—especially in the ears—it becomes a lot more interesting to attack changing chord progressions. We started to hear the tension and release of changing chords as second nature, and as our harmonic vocabulary expands we become more and more accustomed to hearing such changes, and the changes started to provide much of the interest in our solos. Thus, the simple one chord (especially something as basic as the tonic) becomes somewhat boring. I myself once had a lot of difficulty with it.

On one level it's easy, as mentioned, because there's not too much thinking, but on the other hand almost all the interest in your playing has to come from your own creativity, because there really isn't much being fed to you in terms of chords. You only have to deal with one scale, but the same scale over and over gets infuriating fast. Patterns get old, and running scales get old. What can you add?

Well other than those basic elements, you need some kind of raw vocabulary. It is very likely that this is the least of your problems. My life in jazz developed somewhat differently than most. For the first months after getting my first taste of the excitement of improvisation—the phase where we just sit down for hours and hours letting our hands fly around the keyboard, finding whatever sounds easy and feels right on the fingers—I was strangely disciplined about my playing. I had a teacher very early that immediately got me on the path of only playing what I meant to play, and what I knew I would play, rather than just going nuts on the keyboard.

I also very quickly started to explore more complicated harmonic forms, because that's what really excited me at the time. The blues was very boring to me, and so much of the simple stuff, and making the simple stuff sound good, comes from the blues. So this became a hole in my playing.

For this particular type of playing, which in my view is quite a bit different than most types

Cherokee

A couple of great moves in the A section, and some great stuff in the B section. You can't go wrong spending a few hours playing this one in every key. Don't get sucked into playing it too fast though. Start of slow with this one. Clifford Brown could certainly play beautiful lines at blistering speed, but take the time to start slow and really absorb the harmony.

Autumn Leaves—First tune I ever learned, and I'm sure I'm not the only one who can make this claim.

All The Things You Are: Certainly in the Top 10 of most called tunes at jam sessions, this book is a textbook in itself on two five ones, and it has a twist. Rather than start with the ii chord, it actually starts with vi minor.

"All the things" is also commonly used as an exercise in simplification. As will be (has been) discussed, it's often to the improviser's benefit to simplify the chord changes, or to think of an entire section of a tune as a "tonal" or "key" center rather than thinking about every chord change individually. This tune is a great vehicle for such exercises because it spends large chunks of time in different keys (Ab, Eb, G, and E, when played in the traditional key of Ab)—and because the tune is often played at breakneck tempos, the advantages of playing "a key" rather than each chord change has significant benefits.

Take the A Train

Appendix III: Common harmonic gestures

ii-V-I: The granddaddy of harmonic moves in jazz, the ii-V is the heart and soul of jazz vocabulary and should be practiced accordingly. In fact, though as a ageneral rule we aim for balance in our practicing, an entire day of practicing would not be considered a waste if it was dedicated entirely to the practice of ii-V-I's.

I-VI-ii-V: Instantly recognizable "turnaround" that works to bring nearly any standard harmonic form back to the beginning—and it works great for introductions, too!—the I-VI-ii-V is an indispensable part of the improviser's toolbox.

Shift to tonal center to the IV chord of the key:
The ii-V-I is the backbone of jazz harmonic progressions. Learning them in every key, from every angle, is essential. We will use the ii-V-I in

        -- you can play in the tonal key the whole time
-- You can play the modes of the individual chords (but ii dorian is same as I Ionian).

Ideas to Add

In the book, maybe at some point break down all jazz playing into categories. Such as..

7. *Be specific about the chords.*

8. *You don't get any excuse because you're improvising; i.e. what you play has to be as good as anything written down.*

This one more or less speaks for itself. Just because you're not playing classical music, or "art music," doesn't mean that you don't have to live up to the same "expectations" that exist for such idioms. Sometimes we as improvisers get caught in the trap of believing that because of "special" ability to perform extemporaneously that somehow the "other" aspects of our performances can be cut some slack. In other words, such elements as

Arrangements

I think this comes up most importantly in relation to arrangements. So much of the practice time for most jazz players is dedicated to the improvisatory aspects to our playing that, especially among less experienced musicians, the importance of meaningful and well-crafted arrangements is wishy-washy or entirely absent.

It is true that in jam sessions and in music schools one will often find a preponderance of simple "head charts" or "head arrangements," in which the entire extent of the "arrangement," if one exists at all, consists of a decision of which lead instrument is going to play the melody on which section of the tune's form (e.g.: tenor plays A, trumpet plays second A, piano plays B, etc.). At least this isn't literally nothing, but it just isn't good enough for an artistic performance.

9. *Know where you're going to start the next time you sit down.*

10. *__Build__ your solos.*

One of my favorite drummers once said (and I'm paraphrasing here): "What I love about Elvin Jones is that he doesn't worry about 'starting out simple and building a solo.' When it's time for him to solo, he's just going all out from the beginning to the end." This is an apt observation, and it is indeed an artistic and distinctive aspect of Elvin's artistry, but it may just be the exception that proves the rule.

11. *This book is not meant to be gospel.*

This book is not meant to be gospel. It isn't even meant to be true in any strict sense of that pesky word. What it is meant to be is a book that has some rules in it. These rules are written down, and they are printed with some care of pieces of paper. And the pieces of paper are bound into a book. And the book is relatively small, and you can read it, and you can bring it with you.

And if you don't bring it with you, some of the rules—because they are written down and, hopefully, clear and concise—you may remember some of them. Some of them may become something you remember clearly and for a long period of time, something you work into your regular routing or keep as an important goal to strive for. Or maybe some of the rules will irk you, will gnaw at you, even infuriate you. You might think, "Remember that guy who said, 'always have an ending to your tunes'? [Expletive] him." Though I'd prefer to make more friends than enemies, this wouldn't be the worst outcome of this book.

But I think it's a nice thing to have some type of thing to compare against. Some kind of standard to which you can compare. Whether it eats away at you as some type of irritating itch, or it sticks with you as a positive guide, just the fact that it exists, and that I declare that "these are some rules," whether you want to follow them or not, they are rules. I've tried my best to make them good rules. And I've tried my best to make them agreeable to the people who really know what they're doing and what they're talking about. But in the end, all they are is a bunch of a rules that I wrote down and put in a book.

I am not a religious man. Far from it. I'm not looking for religion. But one thing of which I have been jealous in my life has been the beautiful clarity of the rules inherent to most religious faiths. Ten Commandment style rules. Whether you agree with the commandments or not, or whether you agree that the commandments even deserve the title of commandments, what is patently undeniable is that the commandments exists. We all know they do. They are a rallying cry, a standard by which one can compare any other set of rules for life that exists or could at some point exist.

Rules. It's a funny thing to write about, since you don't generally think about rules when thinking about jazz music. In fact, I'm certainly one of those people who believe that standards of right and wrong are nearly the most absurd thing in human thinking. Especially in the arts, there is no right way or wrong way.

But these rules are an effective way to attain a certain goal. As of the writing of this book, I'm not even sure that this is a goal I wish for myself. I think it was at one time, but as of write now no (I guess I'm back at rule #2 right now).

And if you own the book, and if you read the book, and if you come back to the book from some time, it may be able to provide some structure to the overall journey of becoming a musician in the jazz idiom. You may eventually use some of these rules to define your journey. You may also

This is a thoughtful approach to development.

It is one of my primary intents to synthesize some of the wisdom, to my best ability, that I have gained through my training with some of the wisest jazz players and educators out there today. Also, the wisdom that I have personally chosen to weave into the story.

12. Big picture, small picture.

There's an audio lecture series I like called "Big History." It's one of those learn at home deals where some company finds some fancy pants professor somewhere and they basically stick a microphone in the classroom and you can listen to the whole series of lectures. What's interesting about this one is that the framework of the class emphasizes looking at what the professor calls, "scales." From one scale, you can think about your position in history relative to the Big Bang, so and so many billions of years ago. You can look at history from that time to the formation of the first atoms, onto the formation of the first molecules, and so on and so on. That's one story. Then there's the story about the formation of the planets, which can be considered a continuation of the Big Bang story or its own story with some starting point you can not-quite-entirely-arbitrarily assign to some particularly moment in time.

Then there are other stories, like the development of life, then when you look closer at the development life story by itself (putting on hold the overall, bigger picture arch of the universe) you get this other story, which though it is much shorter than the overall history of the universe, is just as rich as the other story.

And the way the course is structured, you are made to "check in" with all the different scales, all the different stories of the bigger history, from time to time. Overall, this particular process of looking at history (one of many) is nice, because the student is made to keep in touch with all these perspectives, rather than get too caught up with the notion of history as something as narrow-minded as American Revolution, or American History in general. (In the framework of Big History, even the whole of human existence is exceedingly minute in comparison to the biggest scale).

I'd like to get a little of this process into the thinking of musicians in general, and jazz musicians specifically. Because it's far too easy to get overly caught in some kind of micro-scale projects (which are important!) and lose track of the bigger picture entirely. Especially with long-term projects, the delay of tangible benefits, or rewards (aka "breakthroughs") can make it far too easy to give up on them. They can also be pretty boring.

The solution to such problems, I feel, is the formation of habits. Such habits must necessarily include such things as daily, weekly, or monthly routines—specific stuff such as precise technical regimens, but also more general stuff, like habitual "reconnection" with bigger picture projects. One of the great benefits of such an approach is the ability to, in some ways, gain respect for and receive pleasure or "rewards" from keeping in touch with overall progress. In this way, hopefully, one

This is a systematic approach. It's founded in the believe that systems are a good thing and that using your mind, memory, and various intellectual faculties to create a framework that will make one's progress more efficient. Yes, I believe in notions such as efficiency, as scientific and cold as they may sound. It's OK if you don't. Many don't. But that's just not the approach here.

I'd like to add here that just because there's some kind of overall scientific feel to some of the concepts here, there's no reason to think of the journey is any colder. No one believes in the more "free" or "creative"—whatever those words really mean—aspects of the artistic journey, but there's no reason at all we can't use methodical thinking to get where we're going in a more direct way. (I should also note, that mindless searching is also a part of my beliefs—but even that can be "placed" within an overall framework of a methodical, efficient approach.)

www.ingramcontent.com/pod-product-compliance
Lightning Source LLC
La Vergne TN
LVHW091153080426
835509LV00006B/667